# The Ultimate Career Guide for International Medical Graduates to Work in the USA

International Doctors' 'How to Guide' to Practice Medicine in the United States

Pathways for International Medical Graduates

The Steps to Take in Order to Practice Medicine in the United States

## Dr Sujan Sen

authorHOUSE®

*AuthorHouse™ UK*
*1663 Liberty Drive*
*Bloomington, IN 47403 USA*
*www.authorhouse.co.uk*
*Phone: 0800.197.4150*

*Published by AuthorHouse  01/15/2016*

*ISBN: 978-1-5049-9478-1 (sc)*
*ISBN: 978-1-5049-9479-8 (hc)*
*ISBN: 978-1-5049-9474-3 (e)*

# TABLE OF CONTENTS

Chapter Three

Chapter Four

Chapter Five

# DEDICATION

This book is dedicated to my parents, Bani Sen and Late Sunil Chandra Sen, who have always been and will always be my inspiration in life.

# PREFACE

There is a growing need for doctors in already developed countries of the world. The USA, Canada, UK, Australia and New Zealand have all recently experienced a shortage of homegrown doctors employed within their national health services. Thus more and more of these services are turning to overseas medical graduates to fulfil their need of doctors. For overseas doctors, working in these countries provides them a better quality of lifestyle. It also gives them the opportunity to receive better training in specialized fields. The ease of modern travel means that overseas employment opportunities are far easier to come by, and this is a key reason why the number of foreign medical staff has increased so dramatically across the globe.

This book gives an overview of the geography, culture and economy of the USA, a guidance on how to enter US healthcare system, medical registration, immigration regulations, ECFMG & USMLE examinations, postgraduate medical training & specialization, residency and post residency and all relevant links to essential web sites. All essential information is collected, collated and assimilated systematically for you. Thus it will save overseas doctors an enormous amount of time, which could be better spent preparing for ECFMG/USMLE examinations and interviews. This book contains comprehensive collection of all the necessary information that overseas doctors will need to work within the USA.

More information is available on my web site www.drsujansen. com. If you still need more information, please submit your query via the web site.

# ACKNOWLEDGEMENT

I am highly grateful to the group of international medical graduates whose inspiration and motivation helped me to write this book. This would never have been possible without you.

I am also grateful to all my friends in USA, who have provided me with relevant up-to-date information to practice medicine in the USA.

# INTRODUCTION

It can be discouraging to read headlines such as one from "The New York Times" in 2013 which indicated that the: "Path to United States Practice is Long Slog to Foreign Doctors".

The article opens with the following comment:

*"Thousands of foreign-trained immigrant physicians are living in the United States with lifesaving skills that are going unused because they stumbled over one of the many hurdles in the path toward becoming a licensed doctor here."*

## Your Pathways

Fortunately, this handbook is designed to help you avoid any and all such "hurdles" in your own path to the medical profession.

Naturally, any discussion of hurdles and serious impediments to success force many potential "IMGs" (international medical graduates) to wonder if there is even a point to going through the often challenging processes required to practice medicine in the United States. After all, medical industry statistics show that one in four doctors currently working in the U.S. had to go abroad to get training.

If American students are going outside of their own borders to get training, why should an immigrant physician make the effort? It helps to understand precisely why the students opt to get training elsewhere.

- Firstly, it is the high cost of a medical degree at an American college or University.
- Second, is because there are not enough seats in medical schools for those hoping to get training and certification. Nor are there enough residencies in chosen specialties for a lot of the potential students.
- Third, there are the demands put upon students of all levels, and these are considered to be very high and challenging due to American licensing standards.

Naturally, it can make it much easier, cheaper, and faster to head outside of the States to get training. However, even when that American student returns to practice their trade in their own country, they may have to still go through the same certification and licensing requirements of immigrant physicians.

Ultimately, every single physician in the United States (regardless of where they initially trained) has to do a proper residency and get the Board Certification necessary for their chosen area of practice. They must do this following a rigorous set of guidelines and requirements. Though this is difficult, it does result in a truly optimized level of skill and experience.

## The Benefits of Meeting the Challenges

So, the international medical graduate - IMG - willing to run the gauntlet of requirements is going to certainly obtain a very comprehensive education and be able to put their certification to use almost anywhere else in the world.

This tells us that the answer to that initial query (*Is it really worth the struggle?*) is a definitive "YES!"

You should also consider the fact that the training opens the doorway to a massive pool of job opportunities as well.

Why is that? The United States is already facing a shortage of properly trained and licensed physicians (which is one of the reasons that American healthcare costs are so much higher than in other countries), and with the new change in healthcare laws due to begin in 2014, it will create an even higher demand for professionals.

In other words, there is a massive job market open to medical graduates, and it is well worth the hassles and challenges of getting properly licensed and certified to American standards.

This still leaves you with the need to know just how to do this (and in the shortest time possible). That is where this handbook comes to the rescue. In the subsequent pages and chapters we are going to walk you through the typical processes by which you can begin working as a medical professional in the United States.

We will help you discover where to look for your residency programs, how to meet the demands of your certification, and even how to develop the skills needed to enjoy and thrive in your "everyday" life outside of work and study.

We will warn you that IMGs face many challenges and that there are a lot of the steps to licensing that seem repetitive for those who have already completed training in another country. You are also going to come up against the entire pool of medical licensing candidates - not just international graduates.

For instance, one article noted:

*"The biggest challenge is that an immigrant physician must win one of the coveted slots in America's medical residency system, the step that seems to be the tightest bottleneck."*

Even when an IMG has already completed a residency in another country (and perhaps worked as an independent medical professional), they are still required to perform an American residency (the one exception is that the United States does consider Canadian residencies as meeting the requirement).

It is imperative that you understand that it can take time and a lot of hard work to make your way through the process, but it is going to be well worth the effort since you will have "top of the line" credentials and a massive range of work from which to choose.

According to Dr. Kevin Pho, "international medical graduates account for 30% of primary care doctors in the United States". That tells you that the process *is* manageable, and that many have gone on to practice in almost every sort of medicine.

It is anticipated that the United States will experience a shortage of 200,000 physicians by 2023. So, if you are ready to begin down the pathway to your medical career in the United States, let's get started! *Register free on the web site (*www.drsujansen. com*) and *get your free career advice consultation*.

# CHAPTER ONE

## A Brief Outline

To ensure that you understand what is ahead, let's just look at the "typical" experience of a modern physician who has immigrated to the United States.

According to the <u>American Medical Association</u>, there are "four steps to practice in the U.S.", but we also want you to understand the secondary steps associated with the four primary ones.

Just consider the following requirements:

1. ECFMG Certification - this is the Certification from the <u>Educational Commission for Foreign Medical Graduates</u>. This is a non-profit organization that looks at the individual, assesses the preparedness for IMGs hoping to enter an American residency or fellowship program, and verifies all of their medical school transcripts and diplomas. They are part of the "matching" process that will align the IMG with the right residency program.
2. Residency Program - Only after the IMG has received their ECFMG Certification can they seek out a residency program. This must be fully accredited by the <u>Accreditation Council for Graduate Medical Education</u> or the ACGME, and it is a relatively complex issue because it will take three years to complete - even if the IMG has already done their residency somewhere else in the world.

Spots in these programs (which can be university or community based) are in high demand (regardless of the area of emphasis or specialization), and this means that the IMG will want to be sure they have clear cut goals, that their English is flawless (as this ensures they will function well in the program and be able to communicate and comprehend everything), and that their background is in line with their ambitions for their American licensing.

Most IMGs will also need to obtain ample amounts of documentation from their residency programs to facilitate future employment (this means letters of recommendation from working, researching, and volunteering in appropriate medical settings).

3.  State Licensing - All medical graduates (including IMGs) must apply for a state license within the states they hope to practice. This can only be done when one to three years of residency have been completed and the three-step medical licensing exam (the USMLE) has been passed.
4.  Immigration - All IMGs who are not already U.S. residents/citizens must obtain proper approval from the <u>U.S. Citizenship and Immigrations offices</u> (which are part of the Bureau of U.S. Department of Homeland Security). What this means is that the IMG must be in the process of transitioning to permanent residency or get the proper work visas (the latter would mean that they have to return to their home country once the training is done).

## Beyond the Basics

Obviously, within the list above are many further issues and decisions to be made. For example:

*   *Where should you aim to do the studies and residency?*
*   *How much can you earn while doing this training?*

- *How, precisely does the U.S. healthcare system work?*
- *Which hospitals offer training to IMGs?*
- *What are the working conditions? What are the requirements?*
- *Are there any agencies that can help someone navigate this path?*
- *And so much more...*

The remainder of this book will cover all of these issues, and in the final chapter we provide you with links and resources to facilitate the entire process. You should consider this information as your primary resource for planning and completing your training.

To make things clear and simple, we'll begin with a look at the United States in general, including the climate of the many regions, the economy, and the cost of living, etc. Then we will consider a summary of the health care system.

After that, we will get into the fine details needed by all IMGs. There is a lot to learn, but we are going to present it all to you in an organized way that will allow you to make the right choices and avoid the hurdles that so often derail an IMG from reaching their goals. For more information *register free on the web site (*<u>www.drsujansen.com</u>*) and get your free career advice consultation.*

# CHAPTER TWO

## The United States

An essential issue to consider when choosing to come to the United States in order to get medical certification is the simple fact that you are heading to a foreign country. And unlike many other countries of the world, the United States contains an enormous amount of land, a huge number of environments and conditions, and a diversity of different cultures. This is not something to ignore or consider a "non-issue".

For instance, a bit later in this chapter we look at the cultural implications of relocating, and that is a very serious matter. Though there are not currently a lot of resources for IMGs in terms of preparing for "culture shock", just knowing that you may be unprepared for such things as the local customs, foods, and even patient or peer expectations is a very good "first step".

Additionally, although the very first factor in choosing your location preferences for your medical residency is the viability of the area in terms of the work and training available, you also want to consider a region that is favorable to you on a personal level too. After all, your residency will last up to three years, so you want to live in a place (and among people) that you actually like and enjoy.

Note that a paper sponsored by the AMA said:

In "selecting residency programs...before an IMG can begin the application process, he/she must select one or more medical specialties. Selecting a medical specialty is best done with the help of an advisor. It may be helpful to consult with physicians practicing in the medical specialties of interest.

Also, IMGs must consider how professionally satisfying that specialty would be for them. For each specialty, it may be useful to research the overall number of positions available, the degree of competition typically experienced in obtaining a position, and the experience of prior international medical graduates, particularly graduates of your medical school, in obtaining residency positions".

What that quotation tells us is that you won't want to focus too strongly on the geographical and regional issues because your primary goal is to simply get the best residency. However, you must remember that location can have an effect on you over the long term.

So, put a bit of thought and research into the process, and you can then aim for the most appropriate residency programs accordingly.

Your decision making process should begin with a general idea of the layout of the United States and the finer details associated with this information.

## Geography for IMGs in the United States

There are nine standard time zones that apply to the United States, with four covering the bulk of the country. There are deserts, rain forests, seasonal conditions, and more than 300 million residents living in towns, cities, suburbs, and many other settings.

This can make it a bit confusing for someone new to the country to decide where to live while working towards their medical certification. As we will continue to emphasize: it is a good idea to focus on a setting that has conditions preferable to you (such as hot weather year round or four very distinct seasons, etc.), but your real emphasis has to be on a location conducive to professional success.

There are some very competitive "markets" for IMGs, and they can be seen geographically. For example, according to the American Medical Association:

- The heaviest concentration of IMGs is in New Jersey (45% of doctors); New York (42%); Florida (37%); and Illinois (34%).
- The top 10 states for IMGs (in terms of the number of practicing IMG physicians in the state) are: New York (35k), California (25k), Florida (20k), New Jersey (14k), Illinois (13k), Texas (13k), Pennsylvania (11k), Ohio (10k), Michigan (9k), and Maryland (7k).
- The "top four primary specialties, the IMG population represents 37% of total physicians in internal medicine; 28% anesthesiology; 32% in psychiatry; and 28% in pediatrics"

So, there are many IMGs at work in many parts of the country, but there are also clusters in very specific states and regions. There are also some pathways and specializations that are more likely to get residencies too. This shows that there can be some competition in the areas with the highest percentages of IMGs, and that there can be a lot of opportunity in regions less popular as well.

You can begin searching for a residency and training based first on your area of preference. Then you can narrow down results by numbers of openings and by your understanding of the overall conditions you will encounter during your years of work. This is why it is useful to have a general understanding of the geography, weather, culture, etc. in order to make a choice that offers professional opportunity and personal appeal.

## The Regions of the United States

The modern U.S. is comprised of the 50 states and 14 different territories (some uninhabited territories among them). It is the fourth largest country on the planet and has more than 3.5 million square miles.

Far to the north is Alaska which touches on the Bering Strait leading to Asia. Far to the west is the state of Hawaii in the mid-North Pacific. Far to the south are nine of the country's territories in the Caribbean area, and far to the east is the state of Maine that stretches out into the Atlantic.

The "contiguous" United States is that which includes all 50 states except Hawaii and Alaska. This makes up the core of the North American continent, which also includes Canada and Mexico. There are, naturally, opportunities for IMGs in the non-contiguous states of Alaska and Hawaii as well as throughout the contiguous region so often called the "lower 48".

The contiguous United States is often seen as containing some very distinct areas and climatic conditions. The <u>U.S. Census Bureau divides the country into several regions</u> that include:

- Northeast:
  - New England
  - Mid-Atlantic (Maryland, New York, New Jersey, and Pennsylvania are located here)
- Midwest:
  - East-North Central (Illinois, Michigan and Ohio are located here)
  - West-North Central
- West:
  - Pacific States (California is located here)
  - Mountain States

- South:
  - ○ West South Central (Texas is located here)
  - ○ East South Central
  - ○ South Atlantic (Florida is located here)

What does this tell a prospective IMG? It says that almost any sort of climate and geography will be available when considering options for training and licensing since some of the "top" locations are found in each region. For example, the Mid-Atlantic region contains a number of the most popular states for IMGs.

This, however, can still make it challenging for anyone to choose a new/permanent/temporary home during their years of study. This is why it may be useful to understand the basic weather patterns of the areas in which most of the IMGs are located (according to AMA data).

## Weather Patterns

The AMA indicates that the top states for IMGs are found in almost all of the regions of the country. This means that all kinds of climates are experienced by IMGs as well.

Generally, however, the "climate zones" of the country include some very distinct descriptions. These are:

- Humid Continental Climate (with cool summer weather) - this covers the northern parts of New England in the Northeast as well as states such as Illinois and Ohio.
- Humid Continental Climate (with warm summer weather) - this covers most of the Mid-Atlantic and central Midwest.
- Humid Subtropical Climate - this includes most of the southern states ranging from Texas and east to Florida.
- Semiarid Steppe Climate - this also includes western Texas, New Mexico, and north to the Canadian border

along the states of North Dakota, Montana, and as far west as Washington.
- Mediterranean Climate - most of California qualifies as this sort of climate.
- Mid-altitude Desert Climate - most of Nevada along with some of Arizona falls into this description.
- Highland Alpine Climate - this constitutes most of the Rocky Mountains region and includes areas of Montana, Idaho, Colorado, and more.

Within each climate will be a range of annual temperature variations, conditions such as rain or snow, and a diversity of flora and fauna that thrive in the environments that the weather patterns, landscapes, resources, and altitudes provide.

This information should provide a useful foundation for those in search of an ideal location for their years of residency and training.

As an example, someone used to a warmer climate on a year round basis may be very unhappy with the shorter and cooler summers and somewhat long and intense winter conditions of the Mid-Atlantic and Midwest states or even the Alpine-like conditions of the northern western states.

Knowing what you can expect throughout the year in terms of temperatures, humidity, and comfort levels is actually a very important factor. Not only does this affect the IMG student, but it may even play a part in the conditions they encounter the most.

For example, one insurance organization pointed out that "California may be known for its health buffs and diets, but studies show that a surprisingly large percentage of the adult population is overweight. About two million residents in this state suffer from diabetes."

This means that any health trends of the specific area should be used as a gauge when choosing where to do a residency as an IMG. In addition to the geography and any conditions common to the area, the economic issues of each region have to be a factor of consideration too.

## Economies

If an IMG student is interested in the economic stability or strength of the region in which they will study and train, or if they are concerned about the cost of living, it is a good idea to do some essential research at the United States Department of Labor - Bureau of Labor Statistics website.

This will provide a state by state portrait of the strength or weakness of the economy. For instance, it is easy to find:

- The unemployment rate,
- The average compensation that workers of all kinds can expect, and
- The general details relating to that region in regards to industry and other economic factors.

For example, if you visit the page for the "New Jersey Economy at a Glance" you can see "Employment & Unemployment", "Prices & Living Conditions", and "Compensation & Working Conditions" for the entire region.

## Using Regional Data to Choose a Residency Location Preference

Why would this matter? Well, there several major issues to consider where the economies of the various states are concerned. As an example, just consider:

- The financial implications on the IMG - Unless you have the financial means to meet higher cost of living expenses, you do need to consider the economic issues of the region in which you will work.

For example, the IMG student in New York or California is quite likely to have a much higher cost of living (as well as steep competition for a residency) during their years of training than the IMG who searches for HPSAs (Health Professional Shortage Areas) with low income populations and lower costs of living in general;

- The opportunities - When a region has a weaker economy, it may end up as an underserved region, and this means that there could be much greater opportunity for an IMG to find a residency; and
- Trends in growth or decline - A simple review of the past and present economic conditions in a state or region will paint a clear portrait of growth or decline in the region.

For example, you can see that IMGs number highly in the large state of Michigan (which is in the top 10), but this is the state that is home to several enormous cities in deep decline. This would not bode well for future employment stability or a dependable cost of living. The data would show the decline and help the residency candidate to make a good decision based on accurate facts.

Of course, the opposite might also be revealed and a city or state with a lot of growth could be discovered by assessing economic and employment information.

Clearly, the wisest thing to consider is whether there will be good options for ongoing employment in the desired field and whether it can meet the cost of living for that region.

## Many Smaller Economies

The United States does not have just its one massive economy but is also comprised of many smaller ones that are far more regional than most people realize. The industry of a state or region can often lead to surprisingly high numbers of medical job opportunities, even if the area seems less than favorable.

A good example of this would be the regions between North Dakota and South Dakota which are currently growing rapidly due to the discovery of vast oil fields. This region has not always had a lot of job opportunity, but is now a major employer - with a higher demand for medical professionals.

Thus, it does pay to do the research and consider the local economies of the places of interest to you for a residency and to discover if they can meet your needs and even sustain your long term goals. This research will also help someone new to the United States to get a clearer understanding of the opportunities, locations, and different residencies currently available.

## Cost of Living

We have mentioned the need to do a bit of research into the geography, climate, and economy of the area in which you hope to live. Another major factor is the total cost of living. Since an IMG is not a student, it is not common for them to receive access to something like "student housing".

Instead, the IMG has to take on the responsibility of his/her own "room and board". This means finding housing, creating a budget by which to purchase food and utilities (such as electricity and telephone service), and also meeting transportation expenses. Because so many IMGs are already certified doctors in their homelands, it can also mean calculating if a location is well suited to the relocation of their family, and its budget and needs.

The good news is that many of the residency programs understand the needs of IMGs and domestic graduates and have various subsidized housing opportunities.

As an example, the New York University residency program has the OCHAP (Off Campus Housing Assistance Program) that gives accepted students access to a special center that is a "resource specifically created to assist in navigating the New York City apartment market. The office is staffed by professionals who provide assistance and information on neighborhoods, transportation options, and other issues related to living in New York City. A small number of subsidized on campus apartments are made available..."

This means that it will be necessary to understand the average cost of living and to accept this as part of the decision making process, but to always give the value of the actual training much precedence over the costs associated with living in the area.

## Acclimatization and Communication Skills for International Medical Graduates

One of the most substantial factors that rarely receive an appropriate amount of consideration is the "cultural issue". Apart from being completely fluent in English, the IMG has to understand the seriousness of "culture shock".

Though someone may have visited the United States in the past, it is entirely different to begin living and working with Americans and physicians from other parts of the world on a daily basis.

This holds true of all situations in which someone relocates to another country, and the different elements of the new culture might come as a bit of a surprise - both pleasant and unpleasant. (It is also why an "observership" is a golden opportunity when available - we discuss these a bit later in the book)

Author Ashok M. Karnik has this to say in his article *International Medical Graduates - Training All over Again*:

"The FMGs [sic.] also face a cultural shock when they start working in a U.S. hospital. Calling a nurse 'Sister' in a U.S. hospital would produce either no response from the nurse or a sarcastic one. Calling a senior resident or an attending 'Sir' may be interpreted as a sign of submissiveness. Remaining silent on the ward rounds and waiting till you are asked a question may be misinterpreted as a sign of ignorance or an inability to participate in discussion. These are manifestations of a polite upbringing or the cultural background of a person; but some virtues, when overdone, may place a person at a disadvantage. While some of these qualities may be so deeply ingrained that a person cannot change his/her personality altogether, a smart resident would make astute observations and adapt quickly."

This is only a small example of what it can mean for someone transitioning into their residency to begin assimilating into the social and professional culture. There is also the simple fact that many residents enter the American system after obtaining "senior" levels in their homelands.

This means that they have left home and all that is familiar, and are often under the authority of people much younger, far less experienced, and who speak a foreign language (English). This too can serve as a major professional cultural shock. To defer to a less experienced person who is both younger and without the same number of years of working in the field can be challenging, and even more so when the overall culture is so new and different.

Simply being aware that many of these issues will arise is a good form of preparedness. After all, it cannot come as a culture "shock" when you have made yourself aware of the social norms, the expectations, and the simple fact that challenges will arise.

On the more social and personal side, this cultural issue is one that might require a bit of research in order to assure the IMG that they will enjoy their years of training.

As an example, the largest number of IMGs in the United States as of 2013 originate from India (the Philippines, Mexico, Pakistan, Dominican Republic, Russia, Grenada, Egypt, Korea, and Italy are the remaining "top ten"). This implies that there are likely to be many Indian cultural resources in the cities and states that contain the highest populations of medical graduates doing their residencies.

However, this does not mean that an IMG will want to look exclusively for areas in which they encounter many similar cultures and peoples as they would find at home. On the contrary, one of the most enjoyable things about living in the United States is the diversity of cultures encountered in almost any location.

Naturally, when someone wants to reside happily in a place for a few years they do need to know if there are specific cultural and social resources available - such as houses of religious worship, appropriate food stores and supplies, and even some social groups that are familiar. This ensures that no homesickness or lack of society leads to an unhappy experience for the resident and/or their family.

They should also be sure they really get an opportunity to experience the society and culture in which they are living and working - without fully assimilating and losing their own background. This can be a bit difficult to manage, and currently there are some resources developing within many residency programs to help IMGs handle such challenges.

Of course, the personal and the professional experiences can vary dramatically. Sadly, the National Institute of Health published a study - "Professional Challenges of Non-U.S. Born International Medical Graduates and Recommendations for Support During Residency Training" - and what the study discovered was a bit disheartening.

Essentially, the report says that four areas of challenge exist. One of them is the "insensitivity and isolation in the workplace" that non-resident professionals encounter. Just consider this quote from the report:

"For IMGs, residency training marks the intersection of immigration, acculturation, and the beginning of training within the U.S. health care system. Existing work indicates that, in residency training, IMGs are more likely than U.S. medical graduates (USMGs) to report experiences of discrimination.

Additionally, IMGs in residency have reported both linguistic and cultural barriers to providing patient care. Many of these challenges persist beyond residency, extending throughout the careers of IMGs. Yet, residency is also a period with existing structure for support, mentorship, and guidance. Therefore... professional challenges faced by IMGs throughout their careers...are amenable to interventions during residency."

So, the news isn't necessarily the best, but the time to use interventions and overcome common problems is during the years of residency. These interventions must begin with the IMG and their advisor, and simply having awareness of the issues and struggles IMGs tend to face is helpful in avoiding or overcoming some of the greatest challenges.

## American vs. Other Healthcare Systems

One of the most common issues discussed in this report is that IMGs felt a lot of culture shock because they were so unfamiliar with the U.S. healthcare system in comparison to that in their own homelands.

Though many had a very broad understanding of American culture from TV, movies, books, etc., they were not so readily prepared for patient expectations, discrimination (from colleagues and patients), and the severe challenges of transitioning in so many ways at once.

Consider the following points from an article about the challenges faced by IMGs:

"In most of the medical schools [outside of the U.S.]...There is greater emphasis on clinical approach...Because of lack of availability of advanced technologies in smaller hospitals, some students are not very familiar with investigational tools such as CT scans, MRI, and angiographies. They may not have seen cases...either due to a truly lower incidence of some of these conditions or because of lack of recognition and diagnosis... Residents from some countries tend to 'talk like a book' because of the 'rote system' of education they have gone through."

This means that a professional culture shock is just as likely as the social one, and that it is best to develop a positive mindset towards such challenges long before they are encountered.

This can be done by relying upon experience and knowledge, but also discretion and tact when doing rounds as a resident and when discussing matters with colleagues. The non-IMGs will have a solid background entirely in the American methodology and approach, while an IMG will have that more clinical and textbook method and experience. Being able to combine these two approaches will tend to make an IMG a far more effective and successful residency physician.

Naturally, this will require time and experience, but as we have already emphasized, having awareness of this requirement will eliminate any "shock" or negative impact it might otherwise cause.

What else can be done? Let's consider that below...

## Using What You Have Just Learned

How can the IMG use this information in their favor? We would like to encourage the following patterns where culture is concerned:

- Seek "peer and intergenerational mentoring [for] cultural and logistical guidance". For instance, get in touch with other IMGs who graduated from your medical program and who have done the same or similar residencies. Ask your advisor for information about cultural and local resources, and use them.
- Be aware of the challenges that IMGs from your native homeland face and seek solutions before you begin your work.
- Use online and social networking to develop relationships with other IMG residents and immigrant communities;
- Seek out and join the ethnic medical associations and societies created for people in your situation (we have a long list in the Useful Information for IMGs section at the end of this book);
- Take the time to study and assess the American healthcare system (we review this with you in later chapters);
- Consider speaking with your residency program directors and those managing graduate medical education to think about policies that nurture an "inclusive and welcoming climate". This could be something as simple as cultural awareness training, etc.
- Use patience, understanding, persistence, and tolerance as much as possible. Everyone has to deal with this same "learning curve" and the more patient and understanding you are about it, the more you gain from any difficult moments or experiences.

## Moving Forward

Now that you understand the "basics" of the United States and how they apply to residencies and IMGs, it is time to move into a more specific emphasis - the healthcare system in general. This is particularly relevant for those new to medical care in America.

As we just pointed out in the last section on culture, many IMGs come from a history of training in an entirely different sort of setting. They may not understand just what it is that patients expect or what colleagues and peers will demand. Because of this, it can become incredibly helpful to have a true mastery of the system for providing medical care in the United States. It is also useful to understand, very clearly, how all medical experts are trained and certified.

Let's first understand the healthcare system in general, and then we'll get into all of the details needed to begin seeking a residency and, eventually, credentials in the field of healthcare or medicine. *Register free on the web site (*www.drsujansen. com*) and *get your free career advice consultation.*

# CHAPTER THREE

## How the U.S. Healthcare System Operates

We already know that (according to the AMA) "IMGs make up approximately 25% of the U.S. physician population." What this means is that around one-quarter of the "physicians" seeing patients are actually in the midst of completing their residency programs and are not yet fully licensed doctors under U.S. guidelines.

However, that does mean that the physician or IMG in question has already been licensed as a physician by an accredited school in another country. They have already been working as an "MD" or something similar to it.

Anyone who is functioning as a physician must have met the requirements established by United States government, and that usually includes a degree from an accredited school and the completion of prior medical training - including residencies.

What is so interesting is that the U.S. should require people from outside of its borders in order to meet current national demands for medical practitioners. However, it is anticipated that there is an ongoing shortage of trained healthcare providers. This all bodes very well for anyone hoping to find a spot in a residency program and to work as an IMG in the U.S.

How is it possible that the country has a shortage of licensed doctors? There are many, many reasons for this, and to understand those means understanding the system in general.

## A Point by Point Assessment of the United States Healthcare System

To keep it very simple, we will use a basic list of points to illustrate the American healthcare system and how it works:

1. Healthcare is delivered through a few channels in the United States: hospitals, medical centers, clinics, and physicians' offices. Physicians can be general or primary care providers or they can specialize, and when properly licensed and certified they can practice wherever there is a need for their services.
2. Most facilities are owned and operated by the "private" (for profit) sector, though a large percentage (roughly 60-65%) of hospitals is operated as not-for-profit too.
3. Physicians can train as primary care physicians or they can specialize. They need only get their licensure (which means that the student met some minimum competency requirements) to work as a physician, but they usually get Board Certification. This means that they have gone through rigorous testing and peer evaluation in order to be allowed to work as a specialist in a very specific area of medicine.

Why do this? Essentially it is due to the higher income available to medical specialists. In fact, a New York Times article about medical training said: "American medical schools are producing more graduates, but many of them will become specialists who can command better pay. The demand for primary-care doctors is expected to stay high, perpetuating the demand for foreign medical graduates."

Both the domestic and international medical students seek to specialize, but a large number of IMGs end up in internal medicine, anesthesiology, psychiatry, pediatrics, and general family practice. This is because the competition is fierce for the specialized residencies, and it is much easier for the international physician to begin working where they find the greatest need.

4. Now, how do Americans access their medical care? They do so through insurance plans or by paying "out of pocket". Americans can get health insurance from their employers or they may have to purchase private insurance. Some cannot afford coverage at all and will visit an emergency room for care when they must.

5. Insurance will pay all or a large portion of the costs of the care a patient receives from a physician or hospital. When someone is uninsured they can pay their bill independently or, as is often the case, they do not pay at all.

6. As in many other countries around the globe, the U.S. healthcare system involves both public and private insurers.

7. The United States is different from others, however, because the private seems to be dominant over the public aspect of healthcare. As an example, a report on the U.S. Health Care System showed that 62% of the population obtained private employer-sponsored insurance while around 15% of the population used public insurance like Medicaid. A staggering 18% was left uninsured altogether.

8. A licensed physician can practice in any setting and access the public and private "streams of income" for providing care through relationships with insurance providers (and by having the proper provider numbers). Many are employed by healthcare facilities, though some also open private practices too.

9. In order to practice as a licensed doctor (MD) in the United States, a physician must:
   a. Have an undergraduate degree (Bachelor's degree) from a four year institution. This degree can be in any area, but should put an emphasis on chemistry, physics or even "pre-med";
   b. Pass the Medical College Admissions Test;

c.  Get a medical school degree that comes from four more years of education (from a Liaison Committee on Medical Education accredited school) and additional training through a residency;

d.  Complete a residency program approved by the ACGME, that runs from three to seven years depending upon their medical specialty (there are university affiliated residency programs and community based residency programs);

e.  Take and pass the USMLE - a three-part exam that is required for a medical license. Though U.S. students will take the first part at the end of the second year of medical school and the second during the fourth year (with the third part serving as the official licensing exam) the IMG will do this in one of two ways:

    i.   Those with degrees from U.S. or Canadian programs accredited by the LCME or the Committee on Accreditation of Canadian Medical Schools will have to register for the U.S. Medical Licensing Exam from the National Board of Medical Examiners.

    ii.  Those with degrees from outside of the country have to register with the ECFMG. They must pass the tests for the states they intend to practice.

    iii. Then, all groups will have to take the final (third exam) through the Federation of State Medical Boards;

f.  Do a fellowship. This is another one to three years of training if a physician wants to focus on a "subspecialty" such as gastroenterology or child psychiatry, etc.;

g.  Once the graduate medical education is received, the individual must obtain their state license to practice medicine. This requires a formal application, the submission of documentation, and a three to nine month "turnaround time";

h. This is also a time when the individual might pursue board certification (which is entirely optional but very helpful to those who specialize and something very commonly done) through the <u>American Board of Medical Specialists</u>;

i. Garner the local credentialing and hospital privileges required to admit a patient to a hospital, work in a hospital, etc.;

j. Receive provider and DEA numbers to work with insurance companies

k. If coming in as an IMG, there is the need to do all of the steps above plus completing the ECFMG process before residency training; and

l. All physicians are required to obtain continuing medical education (CME credits) every year to ensure their skills are current and up to date.

10. Though medical schools are busier than ever, it is anticipated that the United States will experience a shortage of 200,000 physicians by 2023.

This tells us that IMGs of the current era should find it easier than ever to obtain a spot in a residency program. However, there are still challenges and limitations.

For example, "primary care" is becoming less appealing to graduates of American medical colleges. This makes practicing primary care during residency less competitive for IMGs, but as indicated in the "International Medical Graduates in American Medicine: Contemporary Challenges and Opportunities" report from the AMA:

"IMGs...make up one-quarter (25.3 percent) of the physician work force, and more than one-quarter (27.8 percent) of resident physicians. IMGs serve in the neediest communities and are over-represented in primary care specialties."

This may mean that it can be very difficult to get into a residency that will allow the physician to specialize immediately - outside of the primary care specialties, and even then there can be areas where there are just too few residencies of any kind.

Interestingly enough, one article does say that "in a globalized economy, the countries that pay the most and offer the greatest chance for advancement tend to get the top talent," and that many hospitals and universities tend to "cherry pick the most promising young doctors the world has to offer."

Essentially, this tells us that the American healthcare system is already entering into a period in which its healthcare providers are looking for the very "best of the best" from all parts of the world. The universities and hospitals with residency programs are not seeking only to provide the nation with highly skilled primary care providers but also the top specialists of any kind imaginable.

Additionally, a lot of the immigration rules are being altered to allow IMGs to remain in the United States after receiving their licensure.

For instance, legislation has been introduced that would allow people on "J-1 student visas" to remain in the country when their residencies are completed, but only on the provision that they practice in areas where physicians are already in high demand or short supply or when their skills are so outstanding and unique that no one else can fill the need.

This law (to date) has provided more than 8 thousand doctors with the ability to remain in rural American communities long after they have become licensed professionals. However, it is a long way from ensuring that IMGs get the same "value" and employment opportunities as non-IMG physicians once residencies are completed.

So, it is up to the prospective IMG to really understand what they want out of their years of work, and what they can reasonably expect. To ensure that this is as clear as possible, let's consider the issues of working conditions and contracts in the U.S. healthcare system.

## Working Conditions and Contracts for Doctors in the U.S.

The working conditions experienced by physicians in the United States vary tremendously. As you already learned, a physician can work in a hospital, but this could mean they work in the emergency room, in a clinic, in the operating room, in a specialty division or wing of the hospital, and more.

It also means that a physician may work in a teaching hospital, in a hospital designed to treat one area of health, etc. There is also the option for a physician to have a private practice, a partnership with another physician, or to work through a hospital as well.

The conditions can vary from elite to academic, and physicians can find themselves working with exclusive clientele or in areas that are greatly underserved.

However, the entire country is known for having access to the top technologies, equipment, and experts. This makes it a radically different system and overall experience than what is found in many other parts of the globe.

Because there is such an emphasis on "private" practice in the country, however, there are many ways that an IMG may need to consider working in the post-residency period. It must all begin long before the residency ends. One legal expert writes:

"The search for post-training employment is often fraught with anxiety. For an international medical graduate, or IMG, there are extra levels of complexity to consider and negotiate when engaged in the job hunt and interview process.

Though many prospective employers are comfortable with the visa issues for an IMG, others are not. IMGs need to be advocates for them, but also recognize that there may be more limited professional opportunities for IMGs than for non-IMG colleagues.

An IMG and a prospective employer must each understand their respective rights and responsibilities and how they can— and should—effectively work together to ensure an IMG can start employment in the most timely way."

So, as many Americans might say - "the sooner the better" - where planning for future employment is concerned.

## Your Experience

We have already looked, in great detail, at the challenges faced by IMGs in terms of culture shock on the personal and professional levels. This included the fact that working conditions can be very difficult during the residency (and in some cases long after it is done). This is due, most often, to:

- The long list of "stressors" that all residents face - long hours, financial hardships, and the need to constantly learn and absorb new medical information and knowledge;
- Immigration limitations and restrictions (which we will cover a bit later in the book);
- Learning the ways of the U.S. healthcare system, including adapting to the expectations of supervisors, patients, and colleagues while also learning new and appropriate workplace behaviors and practices;
- Language barriers;
- Discrimination (both conscious and subconscious) on the part of the patients, employers, and peers;
- "IMGs are expected to master the clinical practice of medicine. But, despite the shared global knowledge base

in terms of physiology and disease processes, clinical practice often differs from practices in IMGs' home countries because of differences in resources, technology, and epidemiology." (<u>National Institutes of Health</u>);

- A sense of isolation or of unwelcoming attitudes that are often due to simple misunderstandings based on a clash of cultures;
- Pressures that come from the completion of a residency. For example, most IMGs have a lot of anxiety due to the need to search for employment or fellowships as they are still in the process of completing the residency training. The need for career guidance is substantial, but not always available to those with "immigrant status"; and
- The personal costs that the IMG feels in terms of leaving their homeland to provide medical treatment in a foreign country. For example, many IMGs struggle with a sense of guilt while trying to succeed in their residency or new career because they may feel as if they could be doing a lot with their training "at home".

Clearly, this is a lot to deal with as one is still training for a medical career and working as a resident. This is why awareness is a huge key to success.

As an example, if you understand that almost all IMGs deal with this list of pressures, you can begin to:

- Develop peer relationships long before a residency begins,
- You can make plans to use your training "back home" or offer support to your homeland, and
- You can much more easily recognize hurdles as they appear.

Doing these things will easily "soften" the hardships and lessen challenges by providing a pre-established network of support, plans, and guidance.

This will help you to adjust to the working conditions you will face throughout your career in the United States. It will also allow you to focus on your professional goals as you discuss a working contract with any prospective employers.

For instance, you may already know that there are two very common visas used by those seeking to participate in a residency program: the H-1B and the J-1 temporary visas. Within these visas is a lot of room for flexibility and negotiation where employment during and after the residency is concerned.

However, you must know in advance what the terms of the visa (and the residency) actually mean for your future medical career.

Because there are so many ways that the visas can be used to provide an IMG with a permanent status in the United States, however, it is best to have "qualified immigration counsel to assist with the J-1, H-1B and/or green card processes" and "the assistance of health care counsel that is familiar with physician employment contracts." (PracticeLink)

Why? Just because someone is an IMG physician it does not mean that they have any fewer professional rights than a non-IMG physician where their employment contracts are concerned.

Naturally, not all medical professionals will even have a contract. For example, we already learned that there are hospital doctors at many different levels (and pay grades) and there are the private practitioners too. This latter group is self-employed and may not require any sort of contract to determine their compensation and responsibilities.

The IMG physician, however, will tend to need a written agreement that itemizes many things about their residency or their employment.

## What to Expect in a Contract

Contracts must be reviewed by a legal counselor who is working for the IMG, but all contracts should cover the following subjects:

- The responsibilities of the physician;
- Any and all immigration processes that apply to the employment offer and process (For example, noncompeting clauses, payback agreements, and other issues must be itemized in the contract as well as in the associated immigration documentation);
- The term or length of the contract;
- The full amount of compensation for the work (including such matters as bonuses and profit sharing, etc.);
- The "benefits" that include healthcare insurance, vacation pay, retirement income, etc.;
- Termination protocol and provisions - this is a huge matter as most terminations relieve the employer of their legal obligation to the IMG and could bring immigration proceedings to an abrupt end; and
- Itemization of the parties responsible for any and all costs associated with immigration, immigration counsel, etc.

Because any IMG physician is going to be negotiating a contract even as they are still conducting the residency, it is difficult to explore the broadest job market. After all, how much time can be directed towards a search for work, negotiations, and interviews during the demanding hours of a resident physician?

This is why an employment attorney and immigration counsel is so valuable. These two professionals will allow an IMG to enjoy an appropriate amount of "lead time" and planning that will give them a chance to consider the benefits of more than a single offer or opportunity.

In addition to finishing the residency and finding work (while also dealing with any and all immigration issues), all IMGs (in fact, all medical students of any level in addition to all medical personnel) must meet a list of health requirements too.

## Health Requirements to Work as a Doctor in the U.S.

It is "never too late" to pursue a medical career in the U.S., and that means that you can be any age as you seek a residency and licensure in America. You will, however, have to be in good physical condition if you are to meet the rigorous scheduling demands that all residences require.

Additionally, the United States has the "American with Disabilities Act" and it is meant to offer equality to those with "an impairment that substantially limits one or more of the major life activities of an individual; a record of such an impairment; or, the perception that one has such an impairment."

For this reason, most graduate physicians who meet basic admissions requirements for the residency programs in question will be accepted. Of course, there are some cases in which a request for accommodation may be necessary, and it is often up to the residency program directors to determine what is possible and what is not.

## Vaccinations

There are also some very standard medical and health requirements for people requesting immigration visas of any kind, and these are usually limited to vaccinations or proof of immunization to the following:

- Proof of immunity through blood titer to Measles (Rubeola), Mumps, German Measles (Rubella), and Hepatitis B;

- Proof of immunity through blood titer or vaccination to Varicella. Up-to-date Tetanus/Diphtheria/Pertussis vaccine;
- Tuberculosis screening;
- Polio vaccination;
- Influenza Type B annual vaccinations; and
- Any other vaccinations recommended by the Advisory Committee for Immunization Practices (ACIP).

Exemptions are allowed in many circumstances, and these can include for those who have medical contraindications to the vaccination, when a student is pregnant or suspects themselves to be, for those of a specific age, and for religious reasons.

When requesting exemptions for health requirements, it is usually necessary to have formal documentation itemizing the reasons.

For example, medical reasons and pregnancy require an official statement from a licensed physician; age exemptions demand a birth certificate and other official documents showing date of birth; and religious exemptions are usually only granted when a student or candidate provides a detailed (written) explanation of their objection to the demand for immunization on religious grounds.

To work as a resident physician means working through the formal guidelines of the residency program to which you have been matched. These guidelines can vary, but the health rules above tend to be the only ones that you will have to manage in advance of your residency and training.

Another issue, in terms of a doctor's "fitness" to perform their job, and which impacts all medical practitioners in the U.S. is the matter of "malpractice".

## Malpractice Insurance

Medical News Today describes medical malpractice as "professional negligence by a health care professional or provider in which treatment provided was substandard and caused harm, injury or death to a patient." In the U.S., the individual or their family can bring a lawsuit against the individual doctor, hospital, university or other entities responsible for any medical negligence.

Generally, the lawsuit will have to seek compensation for harm or injuries that are the direct result from some deviation from the standard quality of care that the doctor or facility might "normally" provide. However, a study done by the University of Illinois indicated that blood thinners area common cause for malpractice suits as well as drug errors or "missed diagnoses".

This means that residents are likely to face some sort of malpractice issues. In fact, Dr. R. Jason Thurman says:

> "Most physicians would probably say that they expect to be sued at some point, but when it happens, it still comes as a shock...It's important to accept the fact that no matter how good you are and how hard you try, there will be bad outcomes under your care...bad outcomes do not necessarily equal bad care...So if there is a bad outcome, you might be sued, whether or not you did anything wrong."

The expectation that a physician will eventually face some sort of accusation of malpractice is one of the primary reasons that there is "malpractice insurance" available. The National Association of Physician Recruiters explains that there are two kinds of insurance:

- Claims-made - this protects the physician only if the firm offering insurance coverage is the same providing

the physician with coverage at the time the suit is filed in court; and
- Occurrence-made - this is "seamless" coverage that is given regardless of the date of the claim.

There is also "tail" coverage that can be purchased in order to allow coverage to be extended when the physician switches between insurers.

According to the American College of Physicians, "97% of young physicians...are offered malpractice insurance as an employment benefit, but nearly all of these policies are 'claims-made' insurance. Understanding the difference between [them] could mean the difference between adequate protection of your assets and personal bankruptcy."

Fortunately, the individual IMG or resident will not have to find coverage for themselves. Instead, they are most often indemnified by the university/hospital/entity that is providing the residency. This is something that you must verify before beginning the residency or rotation, however, because you could be left unprotected against a lawsuit if the hospital or medical facility is not providing residents with malpractice insurance.

There are a few things to keep in mind about malpractice, however, in order to protect yourself at all times:

- The process is very lengthy and can even take years to be completed;
- It begins with a patient or their family creating the suit, and then any physicians named in the suit will receive a "summons" that the suit is proceeding;
- After the summons is a period known as "discovery" and this is when anyone involved in the matter will give a statement or deposition. This is usually done in a courtroom under the guidance of a judge;

- The materials are then looked at by legal experts, the case is thoroughly reviewed, and a trial is done with a jury. The plaintiff (the parties bringing the case) must prove that the physicians (or others named) did not follow a standard of care and must be held financially responsible for any negative results;
- Many cases are settled out of court, though this is rarely an admission of negligence and more a means of a hospital's cutting costs associated with a court case;
- Because a resident is not making a salary that is anything close to a licensed physician's, it is rare for the case to be entirely directed towards the resident. Instead, it is common for the resident to be asked to testify in such a case;
- If a resident receives a summons, they must visit any risk management department at the hospital or the university. The experts in this department provide all of the advice needed as well as attorneys to handle the matter; and
- Something to remember is that conversations about a pending case should be kept to an absolute minimum. Residents can speak with their lawyers and their spouses as these are protected exchanges, but conversations with colleagues, friends, and other physicians can be used in court. In other words, if you are summoned - do not discuss the case with anyone accept the attorney. If a peer is summoned and you are not, ignore your own curiosity and don't ask any questions because you can then be called to testify.

Remember too that it is entirely natural to feel devastated by the news that you are being sued. Not only are you still in the learning process, but now your self-confidence will take a serious blow as well. Try to keep in mind that lawsuits of this kind are a very common occurrence in the U.S. and that any settlement is never any sort of acknowledgement of a failure on your part.

All universities and hospitals carry costly insurance plans because lawsuits are such a high risk and frequent issue. They even have departments dedicated to dealing with the matter. This is the first resource to go to if anything of this kind should arise. Also try to remember that research shows that residents and IMGs in particular, are not more likely to be the focus of malpractice claims.

For example, the <u>Report to Congressional Committees: United States Government Accountability Office</u> revealed that: "Available data on disciplinary proceedings and malpractice reveal few differences between international medical graduates and U.S.-educated physicians."

Also remember that "not every patient is going to have a good outcome. While doctors understand that that's a part of medicine, they also have to realize that sometimes they are going to be blamed for it - right or wrong. Being sued could happen to anyone involved in emergency medicine. Expect it and be prepared for it. If and when it happens, depersonalize it as quickly and as much as possible. A lawsuit doesn't mean you're a bad doctor or a bad person." (<u>American College of Emergency Physicians</u>)

The one thing to emphasize is that your residency must include malpractice insurance that is paid for by the entity sponsoring the program. If there is no coverage, do not accept the residency!

Having medical malpractice insurance is not something required by law, but it does make doing the job a lot easier. It alleviates pressures and worries about financial ruin and ensures that you are "covered". This insurance is not a credential, but it is an unspoken essential.

There are a few other unspoken essentials to know about where U.S. healthcare is concerned, and one of the most substantial is the "Board Certification".

## Board Certifications

The American Board of Medical Specialties is the first to say that certification is a "voluntary process". However, "being licensed does not indicate whether a doctor is qualified to practice in a specific medical specialty, such as family medicine, surgery or dermatology."

Essentially, the certification is not mandatory, but in reality it is something that a physician would be foolish to avoid. This is particularly true for the IMG who is hoping to receive a J-1 waiver or to somehow negate any terms of their visa that ask them to leave the United States after training.

So, anyone hoping to enjoy a successful career in medicine in the United States must make a point of obtaining board certification. This can only be done after the premedical education, the earning of an MD degree, and the time necessary in a residency program.

To get the initial board certification, the physician must pass an examination given by a board member (there are 24 boards/specialties). This is the initial phase and then the board certification is maintained when a doctor keeps "pace with the latest advances in his or her specialty and demonstrate[s] best practices for patient safety, communications and ethics."

This is known as the ABMS "gold standard" and it is done through their "Maintenance of Certification" or MOC program. This uses customized continuing education along with national standards, best practices, and evidence based guidelines to allow the physician to demonstrate their excellence in their specialty.

The current list of specialties and subspecialties for which the ABMS can provide certification includes:

- American Board of Allergy and Immunology
  - Allergy and Immunology
- American Board of Anesthesiology
  - Anesthesiology
    - Critical Care Medicine
    - Hospice and Palliative Medicine
    - Pain Medicine
    - Pediatric Anesthesiology
    - Sleep Medicine
- American Board of Colon and Rectal Surgery
  - Colon and Rectal Surgery
- American Board of Dermatology
  - Dermatology
    - Dermatopathology
    - Pediatric Dermatology
- American Board of Emergency Medicine
  - Emergency Medicine
    - Anesthesiology Critical Care Medicine1
    - Emergency Medical Services
    - Hospice and Palliative Medicine
    - Internal Medicine-Critical Care Medicine
    - Medical Toxicology
    - Pediatric Emergency Medicine
    - Sports Medicine
    - Undersea and Hyperbaric Medicine
- American Board of Family Medicine
  - Family Medicine
    - Adolescent Medicine
    - Geriatric Medicine
    - Hospice and Palliative Medicine
    - Sleep Medicine
    - Sports Medicine
- American Board of Internal Medicine
  - Internal Medicine
    - Adolescent Medicine
    - Adult Congenital Heart Disease
    - Advanced Heart Failure and Transplant
    - Cardiology

- Cardiovascular Disease
- Clinical Cardiac Electrophysiology
- Critical Care Medicine
- Endocrinology, Diabetes and Metabolism
- Gastroenterology
- Geriatric Medicine
- Hematology
- Hospice and Palliative Medicine
- Infectious Disease
- Interventional Cardiology
- Medical Oncology
- Nephrology
- Pulmonary Disease
- Rheumatology
- Sleep Medicine
- Sports Medicine
- Transplant Hepatology
- American Board of Medical Genetics
  - Clinical Biochemical Genetics
  - Clinical Cytogenetics
  - Clinical Genetics (MD)
  - Clinical Molecular Genetics
    - Medical Biochemical Genetics
    - Molecular Genetic Pathology
- American Board of Neurological Surgery
  - Neurological Surgery
- American Board of Nuclear Medicine
  - Nuclear Medicine
- American Board of Obstetrics and Gynecology
  - Obstetrics and Gynecology
    - Critical Care Medicine
    - Female Pelvic Medicine and Reconstructive Surgery
    - Gynecologic Oncology
    - Hospice and Palliative Medicine
    - Maternal and Fetal Medicine
    - Reproductive Endocrinology/Infertility

- American Board of Ophthalmology
  - Ophthalmology
- American Board of Orthopaedic Surgery
  - Orthopaedic Surgery
    - Orthopaedic Sports Medicine
    - Surgery of the Hand
- American Board of Otolaryngology
  - Otolaryngology
    - Neurotology
    - Pediatric Otolaryngology
    - Plastic Surgery Within the Head and Neck
    - Sleep Medicine
- American Board of Pathology
  - Pathology-Anatomic/Pathology-Clinical*
  - Pathology - Anatomic*
  - Pathology - Clinical*
    - Blood Banking/Transfusion Medicine
    - Clinical Informatics
    - Cytopathology
    - Dermatopathology
    - Neuropathology
    - Pathology - Chemical
    - Pathology - Forensic
    - Pathology - Hematology
    - Pathology - Medical Microbiology
    - Pathology - Molecular Genetic
    - Pathology - Pediatric
- American Board of Pediatrics
  - Pediatrics
    - Adolescent Medicine
    - Child Abuse Pediatrics
    - Developmental-Behavioral Pediatrics
    - Hospice and Palliative Medicine
    - Medical Toxicology
    - Neonatal-Perinatal Medicine
    - Neurodevelopmental Disabilities
    - Pediatric Cardiology
    - Pediatric Critical Care Medicine

- Pediatric Emergency Medicine
- Pediatric Endocrinology
- Pediatric Gastroenterology
- Pediatric Hematology-Oncology
- Pediatric Infectious Diseases
- Pediatric Nephrology
- Pediatric Pulmonology
- Pediatric Rheumatology
- Pediatric Transplant Hepatology
- Sleep Medicine
- Sports Medicine
- American Board of Physical Medicine and Rehabilitation
  - Physical Medicine and Rehabilitation
    - Brain Injury Medicine
    - Hospice and Palliative Medicine
    - Neuromuscular Medicine
    - Pain Medicine
    - Pediatric Rehabilitation Medicine
    - Spinal Cord Injury Medicine
    - Sports Medicine
- American Board of Plastic Surgery
  - Plastic Surgery
    - Plastic Surgery Within the Head and Neck
    - Surgery of the Hand
- American Board of Preventive Medicine
  - Aerospace Medicine
  - Occupational Medicine
  - Public Health and General Preventive Medicine
    - Clinical Informatics
    - Medical Toxicology
    - Undersea and Hyperbaric Medicine
- American Board of Psychiatry and Neurology
  - Psychiatry
  - Neurology
  - Neurology with Special Qualification in Child Neurology
    - Addiction Psychiatry
    - Brain Injury Medicine

- Child and Adolescent Psychiatry
- Clinical Neurophysiology
- Epilepsy
- Forensic Psychiatry
- Geriatric Psychiatry
- Hospice and Palliative Medicine
- Neurodevelopmental Disabilities
- Neuromuscular Medicine
- Pain Medicine
- Psychosomatic Medicine
- Sleep Medicine
- Vascular Neurology
- American Board of Radiology
  - Diagnostic Radiology
  - Interventional Radiology and Diagnostic Radiology
  - Radiation Oncology
  - Medical Physics
    - Hospice and Palliative Medicine
    - Neuroradiology
    - Nuclear Radiology
    - Pediatric Radiology
    - Vascular and Interventional Radiology
- American Board of Surgery
  - Surgery
  - Vascular Surgery
    - Complex General Surgical Oncology
    - Hospice and Palliative Medicine
    - Pediatric Surgery
    - Surgery of the Hand
    - Surgical Critical Care
- American Board of Thoracic Surgery
  - Thoracic and Cardiac Surgery
    - Congenital Cardiac Surgery
- American Board of Urology
  - Urology
    - Female Pelvic Medicine and Reconstructive Surgery
    - Pediatric Urology

Any physician can pursue a path that leads to the background and training necessary to specialize in these many different ways. Obviously, it requires a lot of thought and clarity at the beginning of the medical education process, and also means that any residency has to relate directly to the area that the physician intends to specialize.

## Entering the U.S. Healthcare System

So, what it all boils down to is a very orderly set of steps that a physician must follow in order to succeed in the United States healthcare system.

These steps include the four year premedical degree, the acceptance and completion of the medical degree that earns them an "MD" from a school accredited by the LCME. They will then enter the residency program that is suited to their goals (usually from three to seven years in length). They will also have to pass all three exams contained in the USMLE to earn their license to practice.

They can also do a fellowship following their residency if that will give them further experience in a subspecialty. After being licensed, however, a great many physicians seek their board certification and then create a system by which they meet the continuing education required for that certification to remain in place permanently.

An international medical graduate will also have to do these things but has to pass through the ECFMG process before allowed into a residency program.

Technology changes all of the time, and medical science is something that is far from static. This is one of the reasons that the continuing educational requirements are in place for physicians who want board certification. The American Medical Association says this about re-certification and CEUs:

"Learning does not end when physicians complete their residency or fellowship training. Doctors continue to receive credits for continuing medical education, and some states require a certain number of CME credits per year to ensure the doctor's knowledge and skills remain current. Continuing medical education requirements vary by state, by professional organizations, and by hospital medical staff organizations."

A great many physicians elect to go for their board certification in order to specialize, and as we already learned, being board certified often leads to a higher salary or earning potential.

## Salaries for Doctors

Doctors are high earning professionals; that is just a simple fact. However, even within the medical industry there are huge differences between what one physician earns and what a colleague might take in as an annual salary. The reasoning for the variations are numerous, but include specialization, scarcity of skills, years of experience, research and publication, and demand.

A survey published in TIME Magazine said this:

"Doctors' earnings ranged from about $156,000 a year for pediatricians to about $315,000 for radiologists and orthopedic surgeons. The highest earners — orthopedic surgeons and radiologists — were the same as last year, followed by cardiologists who earned $314,000 and anesthesiologists who made $309,000."

The publication also noted that female physicians earned roughly 40% less than male counterparts and that, surprisingly, doctors in the Northeast earned the least (with the highest wages going to physicians in Iowa, Kansas, Missouri, Nebraska, and North and South Dakota).

Additionally, industry data from Profiles Databases indicated that physicians practicing six years or more tended to earn substantially more than the median salary during the 2011-2012 calendar year.

What is very interesting to note is that more than 10% of the physicians questioned in the TIME article said that they were not rich. Around 50% said they were paid fairly, but all pointed out that physicians begin their working lives at a disadvantage due to the price of their education and the high costs of joining a medical practice.

As Dr. Ben Brown pointed out in his blog "The Deceptive Income of Physicians", doctors must dedicate around 40k hours to their training and an average of $300,000 on their education. However, their hourly earnings are close to the average teacher's and they are taxed quite heavily. Brown indicates that "the U.S. tax code places physicians in a deceptive financial situation."

## Income Taxes

Most physicians dedicate between 40,000 and 50,000 hours of training to become a fully licensed and certified physician. They will spend around $45,000 per year for schooling and graduate with more than $200,000 in debt. They will pay interest on this debt, and yet they can only deduct around $2,500 in loan interest on their annual income taxes. If the doctor earns more than $115,000, even that deduction disappears.

This means that they often don't get to deduct anything relating to the cost of their educations. Additionally, most physicians are not earning enough to repay any significant amount on their loans during their years of residency, and this allows the debt to increase.

When physicians begin earning, they will usually start at a wage that is too high to enjoy a lot of the tax deductions. They will tend to be in the highest tax brackets (around 35%), and this means that working with a financial or tax expert is usually the wisest choice.

When someone is an IMG, the tax codes become even more complex. This is because the tax implications depend on the nature of the payments or income the IMG receives. For example, in an article at FindLaw, it is explained in this way:

"The U.S. tax implications of payments to individuals depends on the character of the payment, scholarship or fellowship or compensation for employment or self- employment.

1. The character of a payment as a scholarship or fellowship is governed by the Internal Revenue Code (IRC) § 117 and the regulations thereunder. The designation of a payment as a scholarship or fellowship by the institution is not controlling.
2. Payments designated as scholarships and fellowships that are paid for past, present or future services are compensation for services.
3. Payments for teaching, research, or other services by the individual required as a condition of receiving the scholarship or fellowship are compensation for services."

This is just a small sample of the explanation of taxes for IMGs, and makes it easy to see precisely why expert advice is a wise idea. Most resident physicians will have to pay taxes, and will have to do so before leaving the United States.

There are many resources for IMGs where this issue is concerned. The residency program they participate in will have staff to offer guidance and support, immigration counsel is often useful for such matters as taxation, and many IMG organizations provide help in the matter.

This brings us to the point where we must begin to actually tackle the "step by step" approach used to become an IMG, and that is the emphasis of the next chapter.

# CHAPTER FOUR

## Becoming an IMG

Let's just take a few moments to reiterate the pathway that is most commonly followed by anyone entering the United States as a resident physician - or IMG:

- Attend and graduate with a medical degree from a college or university appearing in the International Medical Education Directory or the IMED - this is a list of schools developed cooperatively by the Foundation for Advancement of International Medical Education and Research (FAIMER) and the Educational Commission for Foreign Medical Graduates (ECFMG). Only medical schools that have proper recognition from their native governments as authorized to provide medical training and degrees will appear on the list.

(NOTE: Though the schools are approved by their local governments, they are not always "accredited". This makes a difference and a student planning to become an IMG is advised to look at the more formal list of accredited schools that is provided by FAIMER and is known as the "Directory of Organizations that Recognize/Accredit Medical Schools". This is to ensure that their medical degree will be recognized in the United States.)

- Apply to the ECFMG for official certification - This is something that requires two things: first is the medical degree from an IMED institution. Second is the completion of the USMLE exams - including the third exam that provides medical licensing. Only with these two things done can the IMG apply for ECFMG certification.

The annual deadline for certification is February of the same calendar year that the IMG wants their residency to begin. How does ECFMG relate to residency? This certification is the only route open to IMGS who want to use the National Residency Matching Program or the NRMP. Also known simply as "the Match", this is a system that uses an innovative algorithm to identify the strongest residency programs for each applicant.

(NOTE: It is important to remember that the timing of the application process is crucial for IMGs simply because they are forced to endure a full half of a year from the time they complete their graduate work until their residency begins. American students often begin a residency immediately after finishing medical school.)

- Create an ERAS account - This is the Electronic Residency Application Service that "transmits applications, letters of recommendation (LoRs), Medical Student Performance Evaluations (MSPEs), medical school transcripts, USMLE transcripts, COMLEX transcripts (this is only for those seeking a DO or Doctorate of Osteopathy and is the Comprehensive Osteopathic Licensing Examination), and other supporting credentials from applicants and their Designated Dean's Office to program directors."
- Commit to the most appropriate residency - This can take from three to seven years to complete. It must be an ACGME approved program.
- Pursue state licensing or Board Certification.
- Follow through on the requirements imposed by immigration - Some IMGs are issued visas that are active only as long as they are in training, others are converted to permanent residency.

Naturally, this list of steps tells us that the very first thing the IMG has to do is to become a licensed medical practitioner within their homeland, but not all degrees are a alike, so let's take a look at this in order to discover the best pathway.

## Preliminary Training in Your Home Country

If your ultimate goal for getting a medical degree in your homeland is to come to the United States for further training or even for long term employment, you must attend a school that will give you the first qualification required by the ECFMG - a medical degree from an IMED approved school. However, we have already suggested that you take things one step further and be sure that your academic credentials are entirely acceptable in the United States by attending an accredited school.

The FAIMER website has a very useful page dedicated to the DORA, and here you can search by country. For example, if living and training in Albania, you would find a link to the Agency for Accreditation of Higher Education. You could visit that website and find a list of medical schools and programs that have received formal accreditation.

Is it absolutely essential? Yes and no. The website for the ECFMG has this to say about the formal requirements:

"International medical students/graduates must submit an Application for ECFMG Certification before they can apply to ECFMG for examination. The Application for ECFMG Certification consists of questions that require applicants to confirm their identity, contact information, and graduation from or enrollment in a medical school that is listed in the *International Medical Education Directory (IMED)*."

So, if you can only attend a school appearing in the IMED listings it should not pose a serious impediment.

What you might also want to note is that many studies have shown that it can take more than a single application in order to obtain a spot in a residency program. In fact, around 75% of applicants through the American system had to wait around five years before they could become an IMG in the United States. For smooth journey in your career progression, *register free on the web site (*www.drsujansen.com*) and get your free career advice consultation*.

We have already mentioned that some students experience culture shock, and that many relocate with entire families in tow. This is proven even more accurate when you see that the average age of ECFMG certification for IMGs is around 32 years of age.

What that means too is that you should be prepared to practice medicine in your homeland for a few years before you are successful in an attempt at a slot in a residency program. This has its advantages and disadvantages, but is something to accept as a fact of life for modern medical professionals.

You must start with the ECFMG certification. That means first submitting an application, and then passing the appropriate exams. Let's look closer at this issue.

## Getting Started: The ECFMG

All IMGs must first get their proper medical training. They can then make an application for ECFMG certification. This, as already described, is a basic validation of some essential facts. There is also the need to sign a few releases to ensure that the physician understands the purpose of the process.

The next step is the formal "examination" process. This, as described by the ECFMG is as follow:

1. Satisfy the medical science examination requirement. USMLE Step 1 and Step 2 Clinical Knowledge (CK)

are the exams currently administered that satisfy this requirement.

2. Satisfy the clinical skills requirement. USMLE Step 2 Clinical Skills (CS) is the exam currently administered that satisfies this requirement.

(NOTE: These two steps actually qualify as the "three" parts known as the USMLE)

The credentials that the IMG has must also be heavily validated and verified. This means "primary source verification" from the credit and degree awarding institutions themselves, and formal processes must be followed.

Only when the IMG has been fully certified by the ECFMG can they begin "the Match" that will get them to the United States. However, there are a lot of things to consider before jumping into this process.

For instance, we have already looked at the high amount of competition for many residencies, but particularly those that allow specialization. There are also some areas that are just more popular than others and for which many people are applying.

Knowing what you want from your residency is the crucial first step. Ask yourself:

- What, ultimately, is the goal of my residency - apart from licensure?
- Will I get my training and return to my homeland permanently?
- Will I be content to serve as a primary care physician without a specialization?
- Will I immediately seek a fellowship after the residency?
- Am I concerned about where I am working and living?
- Is the income a major part of my path?

Answering these questions can really help you to steer yourself towards the most appropriate residencies, and it can really facilitate your decision making where immigration is concerned.

## Residencies

Becoming a resident, as you know, means getting ECFMG certification, and then being matched with a program that is a good fit to your goals and skills. Additionally, we already mentioned that it can take many attempts for an IMG to get a spot in their ideal residency.

However, there are some "secret tips" for getting into them as well, including these from the Falcon Blog:

"Statistically speaking, the odds are greater that IMGs will match to primary-care fields rather than to competitive specialties such as dermatology, orthopedic surgery, and plastic surgery. Competitive programs almost invariably give first preference to U.S. medical graduates. Since there are more than enough U.S. graduates vying for the open positions in these programs, IMGs often aren't given consideration...IMGs can increase their competitiveness in order to place into one of these specialties or to train at a renowned facility by:

1. Achieving high scores on the USMLE exams
2. Doing research
3. Presenting and publishing research materials
4. Obtaining an advanced degree such as an MPH, an MS, or a PhD

Do keep in mind, however, that if you are hoping for a streamlined method of obtaining a J-1 visa waiver or to transition into an H1-B and then a green card, it can be difficult to do so if you are specializing.

Take the time to actually "map out" the career path you hope to follow. It may not be in line with immigration and immediate long-term employment in the United States. Your residency advisors can also give you very specific information about the limitations that your visa may put on your ability to get into the residency of your choice.

For example, the H1-B visas are far more expensive for the medical facilities to handle than a J-1, and so that too can play a part in just how competitive you are where the residencies of your choice are concerned.

The other tips would have to include such simple things as meeting all deadlines, considering all options where matching is concerned, and doing a bit of research about locations and rates of pay.

As an example, you may want to consider the cost of living and earning potential of physicians who complete residencies similar to those available to you. This will help you to narrow down options and understand what sort of visa to request, what sort of specialization to consider, and which IMG programs to pursue.

Below are the most popular residencies for IMGs, with the area of interest identified alongside the name of the program (if noted by the institution).

## Popular Residency Programs for International Medical Graduates

### **Cleveland Clinic Foundation Program** - Pediatrics
Cleveland Clinic Foundation of Pediatrics S1-12
9500 Euclid Ave
Cleveland, Ohio 44195

**Conemaugh Valley Memorial Hospital Program** - Internal Medicine
Department of Medicine Conemaugh's Memorial Center 1086 Franklin St.
Johnstown, Pennsylvania 15905
Phone: (814) 534-9804

**Creighton University Program** - Internal Medicine
Creighton University
601 N 30th St Ste 5850
Omaha, Nebraska 68131

**Driscoll Children's Hospital Program** - Pediatrics
Driscoll Children's Hospital
3533 S Alameda PO Drawer 6530
Corpus Christi, Texas 78466

**Emory University Program** - Family Medicine
Emory Family Medicine Program
4555 N Shallowford Rd
Atlanta, Georgia 30338

**Geisinger Health System Program** - OB/GYN
Dept of OB/GYN Geisinger Med Center
100 North Academy Ave
Danville, Pennsylvania 17822

**Grand Rapids Medical Education Partners/Michigan State University Program** - Family Medicine
Grand Rapids Family Medical Program
300 Lafayette SE
Grand Rapids, Michigan 49503

**Harlem Hospital Center Program** - Internal Medicine
Harlem Hospital Center. Department of Internal Medicine
506 Lenox Ave.
New York, New York 10037

**Indiana University School of Medicine Program** - Family
Medicine
Indiana University Family Practice Program
1520 N Senate Ave
Indianapolis, Indiana 46077

**Interfaith Medical Center Program** - Internal Medicine
Dept. of Medicine Interfaith Med Center
1545 Atlantic Ave.
Brooklyn, New York 11213

**Jackson Park Hospital Program** - Family Medicine
Jackson Park Hosp Family Practice Center
7501 Stony Island Ave
Chicago, Illinois 60649

**Kalamazoo Center for Medical Studies/Michigan State
University Program** - Pediatrics
MSU-Kalamazoo Center for Medical Studies / Dept. of
Pediatrics
1000 Oakland Dr
Kalamazoo, Michigan 49008

**Keck School of Medicine of USC**
Department of Medicine – Health Sciences Campus
1975 Zonal Ave
Los Angeles, CA 90089

**Lenox Hill Hospital Program** - Pathology
Dept. of Pathology Lenox Hill Hospital
100 E 77th St
New York, New York 10021

**Maimonides Medical Center Program** - Anesthesiology
Maimondes Medical Center Anesthesiology Dept.
4802 Tenth Ave
Brooklyn, New York 11219

## Massachusetts General Hospital
Department of Medicine
55 Fruit Street, GRB 740
Boston, MA 02114

## MedStar Georgetown University Hospital - Psychiatry
Georgetown University Hospital Department of Psychiatry
2800 Reservoir Rd NW
Washington DC, 20007-2197

## Meharry Medical College Program - Psychiatry
Meharry Medical College Dept. of Psychiatry
1005 D B Todd Jr Blvd. Elam Mental Health Center
Nashville, Tennessee

## Miami Children's Hospital Program - Pediatrics
Miami Children's Hospital
3100 SW 62nd Street
Miami, Florida 33155

## Mount Sinai Hospital Medical Center of Chicago Program - Family Medicine
Mount Sinai Hosp Med Center. Dept. of Family Medicine and Community Health
California Ave at 15th Street
Chicago, Illinois 60608

## Mount Sinai Hospital Medical Center of Chicago Program - Internal Medicine
1500 S California Ave.
Chicago, Illinois 60608

## Mount Sinai School of Medicine Program - Anesthesiology
St. Joseph's Regional Medical Center
703 Main St.
Paterson, New Jersey 07503

**Mount Sinai School of Medicine Program** - Department of
Pediatrics
Icahn School of Medicine
One Gustave L. Levy Place
New York, New York 10029

**New York Medical College at Montefiore Medical Center
North Division Program** - Internal Medicine
Our Lady of Mercy Med Center Dept. of Medicine
600 E 233rd St
Bronx, New York 10466

**Prince George's Hospital Center Program** - Internal
Medicine
Prince George's Hospital Center Dept. of Internal Medicine
3001 Hospital Drive
Cheverly, Maryland 20785

**Rochester General Hospital Program** - OB/GYN
Rochester General Hosp Dept. of OB/GYN
Box 249 1425 Portland Ave
Rochester, New York 14621

**Sacred Heart Hospital/Temple University Program** -
Family Medicine
Sacred Heart Hospital Sigal Center
450 Chew St
Allentown, Pennsylvania

**San Jacinto Methodist Hospital Program** - Family Medicine
San Jacinto Methodist Family Medicine Program
4301 Garth Rd Ste 400
Baytown, Texas 77521

**Southern Illinois University Program** - Internal Medicine
Southern Illinois University School of Medicine
701 N First St. PO Box 19636
Springfield, Illinois 62794

**Southern Illinois University Program** - Family Medicine
SIU Decatur Family Medicine Program
250 W Kenwood Ave
Decatur, Illinois 62526

**Southern Illinois University Program** - Pediatrics
Southern Illinois University School of Medicine
PO Box 19658
Springfield, Illinois 62794

**St. John's Mercy Medical Center Program** - Internal
Medicine
Department of Internal Medicine
621 S. New Ballas Rd. Ste 3019B
St. Louis, Missouri 63141

**St. John Hospital and Medical Center Program** - Family
Medicine
St. John Hospital and Medical Center Dept. of Medical
Education
22101 Moross Rd.
Detroit, Michigan 48236

**St Joseph Hospital Program** - Internal Medicine
St Joseph Hosp Dept. of Medicine
2900 N Lake Shore Dr
Chicago, Illinois 60657

**St. Joseph Mercy Oakland Program** - General Surgery
St. Joseph Mercy-Oakland
44405 Woodward Ave.
Pontiac, Michigan 48341

**St. Luke's Hospital Program** - Family Medicine
Medical University of Ohio at Toledo
1015 Garden Lake Parkway
Toledo, Ohio 43614

**St. Luke's Roosevelt Hospital Center Program** - Internal Medicine
St. Luke's Roosevelt Hosp Ctr.
1000 Tenth Ave/Rm 3A-02
New York, New York 10019

**St. Mary's Health Center Program** - Internal Medicine
St. Mary's Health Center Dept. of Internal Medicine
6420 Clayton Rd.
St Louis, Missouri 63117

**Stanford School of Medicine**
Department of Graduate Medical Education
300 Pasteur Drive – Room HC435
Stanford, CA 94305-5207

**SUNY Health Science Center at Brooklyn Program** - Pediatrics
SUNY Downstate Medical Center Children's Hospital at Downstate
450 Clarkson Ave Box 49
Brooklyn, New York 11203

**Texas Tech University Program** - Psychiatry
Texas Tech University Health Science Center
3601 4th St MS 8103
Lubbock, Texas 79430

**UCLA Program for Hispanic International Medical Graduates**
UCLA Family Health Center
1920 Colorado Avenue
Santa Monica, CA 90404-3414

**UCSF Department of Medicine**
Department of Medicine, UCSF
Box 0120
San Francisco, CA 94143-0120

## UNC School of Medicine
Department of Family Medicine
590 Manning Drive
Chapel Hill, NC 27599

## University of Alabama Medical Center-Huntsville
**Program** - Family Medicine Residency Program
301 Governors Drive SW
Huntsville, AL 35801

## University of Buffalo – The State University of New York
462 Grider St.
Buffalo, NY 14215
Program Director: Chris P. Schaeffer, MD

## University of Connecticut Program - Psychiatry
University of Connecticut Health Center Dept. of Psychiatry
263 Farmington Ave MC 1935
Farmington, Connecticut 06030

## University of Kansas Program - Internal Medicine
University of Kansas Wichita Dept of Internal Medicine
1010 N Kansas
Wichita, Kansas 67214

## University of Illinois College of Medicine at Peoria
**Program** - Internal Medicine
University of Illinois College of Medicine-Peoria OSK St
Francis- Internal Medicine
530 NE Glen Oak Ave
Peoria, Illinois 61637

## University of Illinois College of Medicine at Peoria
**Program** - OB/GYN
1 Illini Drive
Peoria, IL 61605

## University of Illinois College of Medicine at Urbana
**Program** - Internal Medicine
University of Illinois College of Medicine Urbana
611 W Park St.
Urbana, Illinois 61801

## University of Miami Miller School of Medicine
Department of Neurological Surgery
1095 NW 14th Terrace
Miami, FL 33136

## University of North Dakota Program - Family Medicine
University of North Dakota School of Medicine - Center for
Family Medicine
1201 11th Ave SW
Minot, North Dakota 58701

## University of Texas Health Science Center at San Antonio
**Program** - Family Medicine
University of Texas Health Science Center
Mailbox 7795 - Dept of Family and Community Medicine
7703 Floyd Curl Dr.
San Antonio, Texas 78229

## University of Toledo Program - General Surgery
Dept. of Surgery
Dowling Hall 3065 Arlington Ave
Toledo, Ohio 43614

## University of Utah School of Medicine - Department of
Surgery
30 N 1900 E
Salt Lake City, Utah 84132

**University of Wisconsin School of Medicine and Public Health** - Department of Family Medicine, Physician Assistant Program
Health Sciences Learning Center
750 Highland Avenue, Room 1278
Madison, WI 53705

**Waterbury Hospital Health Center Program** - General Surgery
Waterbury Hospital Health Center
64 Robbins St.
Waterbury, Connecticut 06721

**West Suburban Medical Center Program** - Internal Medicine
West Suburban Hosp Med Center Ste L-700
3 Erie Ct
Oak Park, Illinois 60302

This list is does not constitute the only options, it simply covers those most well-known for working with IMGs.

Try to keep in mind that there isn't a prejudice against IMGs, but there is, periodically, a hesitation on the part of the programs to work with IMGs due to immigration issues. This is because there are costs, legal issues, and lots of documentation required, and residencies are already fairly competitive with non-IMG physicians seeking out slots.

Each program has its established guidelines where IMGs are concerned and it is up to you to find out precisely how each program handles such issues as immigration, which types of visas they will or will not work with, etc.

## A Few Thoughts on Fellowships

With that in mind, let's take a look at fellowships as well. Though you can use a fellowship to obtain a waiver on a visa and prolong your permission to remain in the United States indefinitely, there are some major challenges in obtaining a place in one. Consider what Dr. Kenneth Christopher has to say:

"A number of the top fellowship training programs in competitive specialties in the US are now not granting fellowship interviews to IMGs. Not because those IMGs are applying from residencies that don't traditionally produce good fellowship candidates but any IMG regardless of where they trained."

This, the doctor explains is mostly financial. Essentially it has to do with the length of time taken to get the certification letters so essential to winning a spot in a fellowship, but also because most visa holders cannot get paid under specific and common National Institute of Health training programs.

Thus, it is the division of the university or institutions operating the study or research that must fund the participation of the IMG. Because, as the doctor says: "Research funding in general is very hard to get at the moment" it can leave the program with its hands tied. And this results in limitations for those hoping to enter fellowships at the end of IMG residencies.

However, there are some specialties where competition is less intense and some organizations willing to look only at the credentials and not at the limitations or costs. So, a good way to begin the search for a fellowship would be to visit the Fellowship Council website, as this is a universal fellowship application and match service. It has a page specifically for IMGs and is an ideal resource for uncovering the best options and the different deadlines for programs.

It will also explain how immigration, visas, and the visa status will or will not impede your success at getting into a specific fellowship. This makes it an ideal time to look closely at immigration.

## Immigration Step by Step

All IMGs have a "visa" of some kind or another. This is not as simple as a visa to come for a vacation, however, because there are so many factors involved. For instance, the federal government actually provides funding to some residency programs, and there are all kinds of stipulations about IMGs in them. This is why you may encounter programs that do not take IMGs.

There is also the fact that a lot of income is earned during a residency, and that the individual is staying for a period of at least three years or more. They might even have an entire family with them, etc.

Writer Eleanor M. Fitzpatrick says it quite clearly in her handbook for IMGs available from the American College of Physicians website:

> "Understanding and complying with immigration guidelines is critical for foreign national physicians interested in pursuing GME (general medical education) training in the United States. U.S. immigration law is governed by specific federal regulations defined in the Immigration and Nationality Act (INA). The entry and monitoring of foreign nationals in the United States is coordinated through strict inter-agency coordination among various branches of the Department of Homeland Security (DHS) and the Department of State (DoS)."

So, it is very official business. Your very first taste of this official business is likely to be when you apply for the visa needed to begin interviewing for residency programs or to take the final USMLE exam. For that journey it would be likely that the standard B-1 or B-2 (business and tourism, respectfully) visa would be used.

This would be a great time to familiarize yourself with the demands for paperwork that are "part and parcel" of the IMGs future lot. For example, to receive that first visa you might still need to gather together such documentation as:

- Registration and confirmation documents for the USMLE exam;
- The letters confirming that you have been granted that residency interview (or two);
- Documents showing your employment or college enrollment in your homeland;
- Medical credentials;
- Financial records;
- The return airline ticket; and
- Any letters confirming your approval for participation in an observership[1] or clerical role at a medical center during the visit.

This list might seem excessive, but gathering this material together is a good introduction of what you might expect in the coming years.

---

[1] An observership is, according to the AMA: "not intended to fill gaps in clinical knowledge or training; it is meant to familiarize and acculturate an IMG to the practice of medicine in an American clinical setting, and provide an introduction to American medicine as they will experience it in a hospital-based residency program...An 'Observership Program' is meant to be voluntary for interested IMGs and volunteer physician preceptors, and should not be considered a mandatory step before starting a residency program." Further details can be found at the AMA Observership website

# Regulations to Work as a Doctor in the U.S.

When you are accepted into a residency program, you have to then get the appropriate visa and immigration approval. Remember that you are going to serve as a physician in training, as a resident in your chosen program, and so your visa has to reflect your status as someone working as a medical professional instead of just as a student.

Because this is a process that can take months, due to the need for an interview and security clearance, you will want to plan well in advance.

You will then have to deal with the second set of requirements for anyone who wants to work as an IMG in the U.S., and these are:

- Name check;
- Forms DS-156 and DS-157 - Application for Nonimmigrant Visa and Supplemental Application for Nonimmigrant Visa;
- Biometric finger printing;
- Security clearance; and
- Payment of all related fees.

Keep in mind that this step provides a visitor with permission to come to the country, but not to participate in any activity for which they would receive compensation or payment. Additionally, this initial visa limits the time allowed in the country to six months maximum.

"Upon arrival to the United States, a port-of-entry official reviews the individual's proposed plan, financial information, etc. and determines an appropriate end date of authorized stay. The date is marked on the individual's I-94 card (Arrival/ Departure Record). Foreign national physicians and medical students must be extremely careful not to violate the terms of their visa status or overstay the dates of authorized stay as marked on the I-94 card. There are serious penalties for visa violations and overstays which can negatively impact one's future immigration options."

This is where things can get a bit confusing, but we'll make sure that everything is as clear as possible. Essentially, when you get a contract for your residency (often called GME training in immigration language), you will have to have the right visa lined up before the program begins.

The visas are usually temporary, nonimmigrant types and include:

- J-1 - Exchange Visitor types; or
- H-1B - Temporary Worker in a Specialty Occupation types.

There are a few other ways training can be done, such as with what is known as an EAD or employment authorization document. This document comes only when the individual has petitioned the government to provide it. They would do this through such paths as:

- F-1 Student on Optional Practical Training;
- J-2 petition;
- Dependent of a J-1 petition; or
- Family of a citizen.

Some even obtain their approval to work as part of a refugee or asylum petition.

There is also the O-1 visa that is known as the "Individual of Extraordinary Ability" visa. This is a viable option if you are a physician with impressive credentials, international renown, and superior skill. Clearly, very few people enter residencies with such acclaim to their record.

## Employer Obligation

Your employer during your residency is obliged to comply with immigration laws and guidelines. They cannot hire you without assisting and understanding your visa scenario. For instance, Eleanor Fitzpatrick points out the following:

"Immigration and employment laws mandate that teaching hospitals pay certain filing fees and assume administrative oversight of foreign national physicians participating in their GME programs."

This is the underlying reason that some will actually limit the types of visas they are willing to accept when reviewing possible residency candidates. Most are very open and clear about their restrictions, but it is the responsibility of the IMG to understand this component of their application process.

Consider that there are:

- Costs;
- Schedules and timelines;
- Regulations and requirements;
- Restrictions; and even
- Institutional policies that will apply to a visa or immigration application.

Knowing if a specific type of visa is going to help or harm your professional growth and options is a vital part of your future success. Though there are some changes being made to immigration policies in order to allow some IMGs to remain in the country after training is done, or to more easily transition into citizens, it is best to understand exactly what your visa can and cannot allow you to do.

## Types of Visas

In the world of visas there are two terms that any IMG must understand:

- Visa - This is a "permit" that is granted by an embassy or consulate of the United States and is a form of approval granting entry to the country for a very specific purpose. The visa usually identifies the immigration classification requested by the visa holder (B-2 for tourism, etc.); and
- Visa Status - This identifies the legal classification under which the individual is given permission to be in the United States. The visa status always identifies the approved length for the approved stay or visit, and it is the individual who must adhere to the terms and dates that are noted on the I-94 card that gives the specifics of their visa.

Be sure that you understand these two items as they are of tremendous importance. During the years of training and work it can be very easy to overlook certain immigration restrictions or deadlines, but this can harm your progress substantially. Not following arrival or departure dates and requirements will appear as a negative mark on your record and can greatly impede employment and access to fellowships or further training in the U.S.

One you make note of the specifics of a visa, just be sure to work with your residency program director to meet any and all requirements. These vary according to the visa granted. The types of visas most commonly used by IMGs are:

- ECFMG Sponsorship and a J-1 Exchange Visa Program - This is the most common visa that IMGs will use. Essentially, the U.S. Department of State has given the ECFMG the right to sponsor IMGs through J-1 visas.

Naturally, to get this visa you must pass the USMLE exams, have a valid ECFMG certificate (there are expiration dates on their certifications), have an official offer from a residency program, and a letter from the Ministry of Health (or its equivalent) of your place of legal residence.

This, however, is also the visa that includes the "two year home country physical presence requirement". In other words, when the training is done, you will be obligated to go back to your homeland for a period of at least two years in order to share the knowledge gained in your training.

This is also the type of visa requirement that is being altered in order to allow some to avoid the two-year return. These are "J-1 waivers" that include:

- o If the individual can prove they will endure persecution in their homeland;
- o If the requirement would force hardship on the spouse or children of the individual because they are U.S. residents; and
- o If the individual has sponsorship from an "interested governmental agency" or IGA that wants them to remain in the country. (This is the most common route that an IMG receives a waiver of the return requirement - as an example, the VA or Department of Veterans Affairs may sponsor a physician who is providing care in a location that is underserved by medical professionals, etc.)
- • H-1B Temporary Worker visas - This is a bit more complex than the J-1 because it is for temporary workers in "specialty occupations". For IMGs to get this they must pass the FLEX (or a similar exam, passes a rigorous English exam, and already is licensed in their area of expertise.

Why use this? There is no two year home residence requirement, and it allows someone to enter the country and work at the professional level for a period of up to six years.

This is an "employer specific" visa, and that mean that the IMG must be the recipient of a special petition filed by their residency program. To get an approval on that petition the IMG must have an unrestricted state medical license, an MD or unrestricted foreign medical license, passage of the rigorous ECFMG English exam, and complete passage of all three USMLE exams.

This visa also has a few waivers and variations. These include the F-1 Student Optional Practical Training that is similar to H-1B with the exception that it requires the individual to have a prearranged job, and to start with an initial cap of three years that can be extended another three if needed. Then they must be outside of the U.S. for one year before they can re-enter.

There is also the H-3 visa for any trainee who cannot get similar training in their homeland. This is a very rigid visa that requires the individual to return home and use the skills gained under their U.S. studies.

- Immigrant visas - Also known as "green cards", these give someone permission to permanently remain in the United States. They can then become full "naturalized" citizens after remaining in the country for three to five years.

Getting immigrant status demands that the IMG be specified as an employee of a sponsoring entity. This status can be revoked should the IMG fall into a list of categories that are not allowable under U.S. law.

How does all of this actually "work" for the IMG? Let's use a very simple illustration.

## A Basic Visa Immigration Illustration

A woman doing a residency in the U.S. enters on a J-1 visa. She does her residency in an underserved area and is given a waiver. She has a state medical license and a new work authorized visa status that enables her to consider requesting an H-1B visa or even an immigrant visa. This would be filed with the Department of Labor, and perhaps the Immigration and Naturalization Service.

This would be an ideal way to remain in the country, but one report from the American Medical Association has this to say as well:

"There are several different options for IMGs wishing to become permanent residents in the U.S...based on the national interest waiver classification. That is, IMGs whose continued residence and employment in the U.S. benefited the national interest, for example by working in an underserved community, qualified for an expedited permanent residency process. However, many physicians do not qualify for residency based on a national interest waiver... [so] obtaining permanent resident status becomes a much more arduous process."

This means that permanent status has to be considered very carefully. An employer can use the labor certification process that shows that the IMG is not harmful to the labor pool available in the country and that they are the only candidate qualified for the position they will be hired to fill.

To obtain this requires a lot of documentation and a formal approval from the Department of Labor. After that, the employer will submit the Immigrant Visa Petition and then the IMG would have to apply for permanent residence through the consulate in their homeland or through the INS.

Of course, the "Aliens of Extraordinary Ability or for Outstanding Professors or Researchers" is a final method. As we already said, however, it is rarely put to use because of the mountain of evidence necessary to prove this is the case.

## Post Training Issues

Though you are already aware of a tremendous list of "must do" issues that will have to occur even as you work in the residency program, the "post training" period has to be handled too - especially where your visa is concerned.

Fortunately, we have already identified the most common ways that you might approach this part of your career:

- J-1 visas - You already know that you can get a waiver of some sort, but we did not yet point out the "physician shortage areas" that also apply. These allow the individual to get a waiver of their two year return obligation by agreeing to work in areas officially noted as being shortage areas where healthcare is concerned.

Additionally, a resident physician with this visa, and who is participating in a fellowship at the end of the residency can remain in the U.S. on their visa.

- National Interest Waivers - We did also mention the NIWs, which provide the IMG the opportunity to gain permanent residence when they commit to a five year contract in a physician shortage area after they have completed their residency.

The ways that waivers work for employment are pretty specific. The J-1 waivers tend to be mostly made available for primary care physicians as the entire waiver program was created to fill national gaps in primary care coverage.

You can get in touch with the following sponsoring agencies to explore your options for such waivers:

- Any State Department of Public Health
- Department of Health and Human Services - applies to primary care physicians and biomedical researchers
- Veterans Administration - has more than 170 facilities
- Appalachian Regional Commission (ARC)

## Challenges to Anticipate

If you are pursuing a fellowship or some specialty outside of primary care, it is going to be very challenging to get a job to free you of the visa requirement to return home once the fellowship or residency come to an end.

However, don't give up just yet because specialist waivers can be obtained from the resources just mentioned above.

These do have their strict rules, however, and these include the need to work in an HPSA - Health Professional Shortage Area. These are found in very rural areas but also in many inner-city settings. Most of the waivers demand a three year commitment, and will change the visa from a J-1 to an H-1B. When the requirements are met, the individual becomes eligible for their green card.

So, if you are willing to make a commitment of three or more years and to focus on the most in demand areas of medical practice (usually primary care, internal medicine, psychiatry, pediatrics, or anesthesiology) the waiver system may be a good way to secure employment.

Resources and complete information about the many HPSA locations can be found at the United States Department of Health and Human Services HRSA website.

Remember too that in addition to handling the visa issues as the residency nears its end, those who want to remain in the

United States have to be sure that they can get proper state licensure.

## State Licensing 101

As you near the completion of the residency and begin to plan your future, it often means looking for work. To do this, however, means having the appropriate medical licensure. Unfortunately, each state has different requirements and so it can be a bit confusing.

The general demands prior to gaining a state license are very standard. You must first have your ECFMG certification. You have to have done the residency in an ACGME approved program. You will then have to have a set number of post graduate training years as an IMG and you cannot have exceeded the number of attempts at the USMLE third part exam. Below is a summary of the state guidelines from the American Medical Association:

| | Years in Residency before Test 3 of USMLE is Allowed | Number of Years in IMG Program for Licensure |
| --- | --- | --- |
| Alabama | 2 yrs | 3 yrs |
| Alaska | 1 yr | 3 yrs |
| Arizona | 6 mos. | 3 yrs |
| Arkansas | none | 3 yrs |
| California | None | 2 yrs (including 4 mos general med) |
| Colorado | 3 yrs | 3 yrs |
| Connecticut | None | 2 yrs |
| Delaware | 1 yr | 3 yrs |
| DC | 3 yrs | 3 yrs |
| Florida | None | 2 yrs |
| Georgia | 1-3 yrs | 3 yrs |
| Hawaii | 1 yr | 2 yrs |

| Idaho | 2 yrs 9 mos | 3 yrs |
|---|---|---|
| Illinois | 1 yr | 1 yr (entered GME pre-1988) OR 2 yrs (entered GME post –1988) |
| Indiana | 2 yrs | 2 yrs |
| Iowa | 7 mos (or enrollment in GME prgm approved by board at time of application for Step 3) | 2 yrs |
| Kansas | 2 yrs or enrollment in GME program in Kansas | 2 yrs |
| Kentucky | 1 yr | 2 yrs |
| Louisiana | None | 3 yrs (fifth pathway may be counted as 1 yr of required GME) |
| Maine | 1 yr | 3 yrs |
| Maryland | None (1 yr if 3 fails in any step) | 2 yrs AOA- or ACGME-accred GME as of 10/2000 |
| Massachusetts | 1 yr | 2 yrs |
| Michigan | 6 mos | 2 yrs |
| Minnesota | None (must be enrolled in GME) | 2 yrs |
| Mississippi | 1 yr | 3 yrs (or 1 yr plus ABMS certification) |
| Missouri | 3 yrs | 3 yrs |
| Montana | 3 yrs | 3 yrs (or ABMS or AOA certification) |
| Nebraska | None | 3 yrs |
| Nevada | None | 3 yrs |
| New Hampshire | 1 yr | 2 yrs |
| New Jersey | 1 yr | 3 yrs (1 yr if medical school completed before 7/1/85; 2yrs, and contract for year 3, if graduated after July 1, 2003) |
| New Mexico | 1 yr | 2 yrs |
| New York | None | 3 yrs |
| North Carolina | 3 yrs (none if enrolled in state) | 3 yrs |

| North Dakota | 1 yr (none if enrolled in state) | 3 yrs |
|---|---|---|
| Ohio | 9 mos | 2 yrs (through the 2nd year level) |
| Oklahoma | none | 2 yrs |
| Oregon | none (must be in GME program) | 3 yrs |
| Pennsylvania | None | 3 yrs (1 yr if GME taken in US before 7/87) |
| Puerto Rico | None | 3 yrs |
| Rhode Island | 1 yr | 3 yrs |
| South Carolina | 3 yrs | 3 yrs |
| South Dakota | 1 yr | Completion of residency(1 yr if US GME taken before 7/87) |
| Tennessee | 1 yr | 3 yrs |
| Texas | None | 3 yrs |
| Utah | None | 2 yrs |
| Vermont | 7 mos | 3 yrs (Canadian GME not accepted) |
| Virginia | None | 2 yrs |
| Washington | 1 yr | 2 yrs (1 yr if medical school completed before 7/28/85) |
| West Virginia | None | 3 yrs (or 1 yr plus ABMS certification) |
| Wisconsin | 1 yr | 1 yr |
| Wyoming | 2 yrs | 2 yrs |

Traditionally a program advisor will walk the IMG through this process as it tends to be part of the residency. However, this is not always the case. Many IMGs tend to hire legal counsel to facilitate the planning process and to ensure that their residency provides them with the desired end result.

As we have emphasized many times throughout this book, it is really all a matter of good planning and thoughtful consideration before the training even begins. Asking yourself about your goals will help you to make all of the necessary arrangements, meet the many different deadlines, and know when it is time for you to seek licensure and any other formal documents or essentials.

## In Conclusion

This brings us to the end of the step by step and "how to" parts of the book. With this information you will be able to make the plans necessary to get the best education, take all of the right steps, and find a residency that provides you with the training you need to reach your goals.

In the next and final chapter we are going to provide the many resources mentioned throughout this book, and which will enable you to become an IMG and even a citizen in the United States.

This chapter includes links to recruiters and job resources, but also the ethnic medical societies that can help you with professional and personal success and all of the organizations needed to become an IMG.

Throughout the chapters you have learned about the challenges faced by IMGs and how to overcome them, or prepare for them accordingly. Please be sure to put all of links to use as they are invaluable to most people who have not lived and worked in the United States in the past. The different societies and organizations mentioned will really help you to meet all of the official demands as well as feeling confident and comfortable in what is, for many, a totally foreign and competitive environment. *Register free on the web site* (www. drsujansen.com) and *get your free career advice consultation.*

Good luck with your training.

# CHAPTER FIVE

## Useful Information for IMGs

**List of Essential Resources**

Education

- International Medical Education Directory or the IMED
- DORA - Directory of Organizations that Recognize/ Accredit Medical Schools

Immigration

- U.S. Citizenship and Immigrations
- American Medical Association Department of IMG Services

USMLE and Exams

- United States Medical Licensing Examination (USMLE)
- National Board of Medical Examiners

Residency

- Educational Commission for Foreign Medical Graduates (ECFMG)
- Accreditation Council for Graduate Medical Education

- National Residency Matching Program
- AMA Observership
- Electronic Residency Application Service

## Specialization

- Federation of State Medical Boards of the U.S.
- American Board of Medical Specialists

## Post-Residency

- Fellowship Council website
- Medically Underserved Resources at U.S. Department of Health and Human Services
- Bureau of Primary Health Care - resource for Healthcare Provider Shortage Areas information
- Veterans Administration
- Indian Health Service
- U.S. Department of State
- Appalachian Regional Commission
- National Rural Recruitment and Retention Network

## Immigration Legal Counsel (Recommended by the AMA)

- American Immigration Lawyers Association - (800) 982-2839
- The Law Offices of Carl Shusterman - (213) 623-4592
- Immigration Law Associates, P.C. - (847) 763-8500
- Ingber and Aronson Immigration Law Firm - (612) 339-0517
- Suskind Susser - (901) 682-6455
- True, Walsh & Miller, LLP - (607) 273-4200

- <u>Rubman & Harris, LLC</u> - (312) 341-1907
- <u>Stinson Morrison Hecker LLP</u> - (314) 863-0800

## Recruiters Known to Work with IMGs

- <u>Alliance of Medical Recruiters</u>
- <u>Association of Staff Physician Recruiters</u>
- <u>Enterprise Medical Services</u>
- <u>McCall & Lee</u>
- <u>MD Resources, Inc.</u>
- <u>Merritt Hawkins</u>
- <u>National Association of Physician Recruiters</u>
- <u>Olesky Associates, Inc.</u>
- <u>Pacific Companies</u>
- <u>Rural Recruitment and Retention Network</u>
- <u>Worldwide Medical Services</u>

## Private Medical Recruitment Agencies

The National Association of Physician Recruiters offers the following private agencies on a state by state basis:

| Recruitment Firm | State |
|---|---|
| CRAssociates, Inc. | Alabama |
| D&Y | Alabama |
| East Alabama Medical Center | Alabama |
| Gammons Group, Inc. | Alabama |
| Lanier Medical Placement LLC | Alabama |
| Conway Regional Medical Center | Arkansas |
| Washington Regional Medical Center | Arkansas |
| AB Staffing Solutions LLC | Arizona |
| Banner Health | Arizona |
| Catalina Medical Recruiters, Inc. | Arizona |
| Franklin Joseph & Associates | Arizona |
| Bosley | California |

| | |
|---|---|
| California Physician Opportunities | California |
| Carson Kolb Healthcare Group, Inc | California |
| EmCare, Inc. | California |
| Fidelis Partners | California |
| Saint Louise Regional Hospital | California |
| Solvere | California |
| Sonora Regional Medical Center | California |
| Conifer Physician Resources | Colorado |
| Conovan Healthcare Recruitment, LLC | Colorado |
| Mountain Medical Group | Colorado |
| Rocky Mountain Medical Search | Colorado |
| Alpha Medical Group | Connecticut |
| Beacon Physician Placement Services | Connecticut |
| EOS Healthcare Solutions Inc. | Connecticut |
| HealthField Alliance, The | Connecticut |
| Onward MD | Connecticut |
| ProMedical Staffing LLC | Connecticut |
| Stratton Group, LLC | Connecticut |
| Teed & Company | Connecticut |
| Christiana Care Health System | Delaware |
| 1888MDSEARCH, Inc. | Florida |
| 21st Century Oncology, LLC | Florida |
| All Care Consultants, Inc. | Florida |
| All Star Recruiting Inc | Florida |
| American Medical Consultants, Inc. | Florida |
| American Physician Network, Inc. | Florida |
| Anthem Associates | Florida |
| Atlantic MEDsearch, Inc. | Florida |
| Bancosh Associates LLC | Florida |
| Baptist Health South Florida | Florida |
| Born & Bicknell, Inc. | Florida |
| CCL Medical Search | Florida |
| Central Florida Health Alliance | Florida |
| EDGE Physicians | Florida |
| Fairway Recruiting | Florida |

| | |
|---|---|
| Hayes Locums | Florida |
| Herman Medical Staffing GmbH | Florida |
| Integrity Healthcare | Florida |
| Luke & Associates | Florida |
| MASC Medical Recruitment Firm | Florida |
| MDR Associates | Florida |
| Medical Consultants of America, Inc. | Florida |
| Mednax National Medical Group | Florida |
| National Health Partners, Inc. | Florida |
| National Health Resources Inc dba NHR | Florida |
| National Locum Tenens, LLC | Florida |
| National Staffing Solutions | Florida |
| Phoenix Physicians, LLC | Florida |
| Resolute Healthcare | Florida |
| RSPA | Florida |
| Spot On Recruiting, Inc. | Florida |
| TIVA HealthCare, Inc. | Florida |
| Vantage Search Group, Inc. | Florida |
| ApolloMD | Georgia |
| Boone-Scaturro Associates, Inc. | Georgia |
| Calvert Medical Associates | Georgia |
| Ericksson Associates | Georgia |
| Executive Clinical Services, LLC | Georgia |
| MD moving | Georgia |
| Nelson James & Associates | Georgia |
| Pinnacle Health Group | Georgia |
| Southeast Physician Search | Georgia |
| St. Francis Hospital | Georgia |
| The Hart Group, Ltd. | Georgia |
| The Stembridge Agency, LLC | Georgia |
| Ursula Thomas & Assoc | Georgia |
| Acute Care, Inc. | Iowa |
| Apogee Physicians | Idaho |
| Adkisson Consultants, Inc | Illinois |
| Dovetail Recruiting, LLC | Illinois |

| | |
|---|---|
| Locum MD-LLC | Illinois |
| M.J. Jones & Associates | Illinois |
| MedAscend LLC | Illinois |
| OSF HealthCare | Illinois |
| Priority Physicians, Inc. | Illinois |
| Quincy Medical Group | Illinois |
| Stratum Med | Illinois |
| Vein Clinics of America | Illinois |
| Good Samaritan Hospital (IN) | Indiana |
| Harrison County Hospital | Indiana |
| PracticewiseM.D. | Indiana |
| St. Vincent Medical Group | Indiana |
| Docs Who Care | Kansas |
| Physicians Search, Inc. | Kansas |
| Priority Physician Placement | Kansas |
| Sherriff & Associates, Inc. | Kansas |
| Steele Healthcare Solutions | Kansas |
| CHC | Kentucky |
| FCS, Inc. | Kentucky |
| Mountain After Hours Clinic PSC | Kentucky |
| MD Staff Pointe, LLC | Louisiana |
| Med Tracker Personnel, LLC | Louisiana |
| Physician & Healthcare Resource Group | Louisiana |
| Primary Health Services Center | Louisiana |
| Teche Regional Medical Center | Louisiana |
| Hope Health, Inc. | Massachusetts |
| Olesky Associates Inc. | Massachusetts |
| Bridge4MDs, LLC | Maryland |
| Erickson Health Medical Group | Maryland |
| University of Maryland Medical System | Maryland |
| Health Search New England | Maine |
| MOUNTAIN, LTD. | Maine |
| Confidential MD, Inc. | Michigan |
| Emergency Consultants, Inc. | Michigan |
| Otsego Memorial Hospital | Michigan |

| | |
|---|---|
| Recruitment Management Systems | Michigan |
| Stackpoole & Associates, LLC | Michigan |
| Whitney Recruitment, LLC | Michigan |
| CareerStaff Unlimited | Missouri |
| Cejka Search | Missouri |
| Enterprise Medical Services | Missouri |
| Interim Physicians, LLC | Missouri |
| Jordan Medical Consultants | Missouri |
| KCMedNet | Missouri |
| KPS Physician Staffing | Missouri |
| MediaCross, Inc. | Missouri |
| PHYSICIAN e-CRUIT | Missouri |
| Sante Consulting, LLC | Missouri |
| Source Medical | Missouri |
| SoutheastHEALTH | Missouri |
| The Toberson Group | Missouri |
| Trouveer Associates, Inc. | Missouri |
| Webber and Company | Missouri |
| Memorial Hospital at Gulfport | Mississippi |
| Carolina Family Medicine & Urgent Care | North Carolina |
| Carolinas HealthCare System | North Carolina |
| Coors Healthcare Solutions | North Carolina |
| Intelligent Placement Solutions | North Carolina |
| Medical Career Consultants, LLC | North Carolina |
| Medstaff National Medical Staffing | North Carolina |
| Open Door Unlimited, Inc. | North Carolina |
| Search Resource Group, LLC | North Carolina |
| WakeMed Health and Hospitals | North Carolina |
| Wilson Medical Center | North Carolina |
| National Medical Resources (NMR) | North Dakota |
| Aureus Medical Group | Nebraska |
| Core Physicians, LLC | New Hampshire |
| Elliot Health System | New Hampshire |
| Emergency Medical Associates Inc. of NJ NY | New Jersey |
| Medical Search International | New Jersey |

| | |
|---|---|
| Princeton House Behavioral Health | New Jersey |
| Summit Recruiting Group, LLC | New Jersey |
| TeamHealth | New Jersey |
| San Juan Regional Medical Center | New Mexico |
| 1FocusLocums.US, LLC | Nevada |
| St. Rose Dominican Hospital | Nevada |
| Adirondack Medical Center | New York |
| Advanced Medical Personnel | New York |
| Akita Staffing Group, LLC | New York |
| Blackwell Associates, Inc. | New York |
| Durham Medical Staffing | New York |
| Harris Brand Recruiting | New York |
| International Medical Placement, Ltd | New York |
| Physician Affiliate Group of New York, P.C. | New York |
| Professional Placement Associates Inc. | New York |
| River Medical Recruiting Inc. | New York |
| St. Luke's Cornwall Hospital | New York |
| Stanton Healthcare Group | New York |
| Winston Resources | New York |
| Advantage Locums, LLC | Ohio |
| Annashae Corporation | Ohio |
| Humility of Mary Health Partners | Ohio |
| Ohio State University Medical Center, The | Ohio |
| Physician Staffing, Inc. | Ohio |
| Randstad Healthcare | Ohio |
| RosmanSearch, Inc. | Ohio |
| AIM Consultants | Oklahoma |
| Care ATC, Inc. | Oklahoma |
| The Clements Group, LLC | Oklahoma |
| Asante Physician Partners | Oregon |
| Altoona Internal Medicine PA | Pennsylvania |
| B.E.L. & Associates, Inc. | Pennsylvania |
| Healthcare Recruitment Counselors | Pennsylvania |
| Intensivist Jobs | Pennsylvania |
| Lawlor & Associates, Inc. | Pennsylvania |

| | |
|---|---|
| Lehigh Valley Health Network | Pennsylvania |
| Rogo Search, The Physician Source | Pennsylvania |
| A Berendt Associates, Inc. | South Carolina |
| Palmetto Health | South Carolina |
| Self Regional Healthcare | South Carolina |
| Cumberland Medical Center | Tennessee |
| HCA Healthcare | Tennessee |
| LifePoint Hospitals, Inc. | Tennessee |
| Seaboard Healthcare | Tennessee |
| Siskind Susser | Tennessee |
| Adaptive Medical Partners (AMP-Health, Inc.) | Texas |
| Alliance Recruiting Resources, Inc. | Texas |
| Arthur, Marshall Inc. | Texas |
| ATC Physician Services | Texas |
| Beck-Field & Associates, Inc. | Texas |
| BSM Business Solutions Management, Inc. | Texas |
| Byron Locums | Texas |
| Concentra | Texas |
| Delta Companies, The | Texas |
| Easter Medical Staffing | Texas |
| Eskridge & Associates | Texas |
| Falcon HCA, Inc. | Texas |
| Finders Firm, LLC | Texas |
| Goldfish Partners | Texas |
| Good Shepherd Medical Center (TX) | Texas |
| Hendrick Medical Center | Texas |
| Maxim Physician Resources | Texas |
| Medical Search | Texas |
| Mint Physician Staffing | Texas |
| Novus Medical, LLC | Texas |
| Pediatric Search Partners | Texas |
| Practice Dynamics, Inc. | Texas |
| Professional Performance Development Group, Inc. | Texas |
| SourceMD, Inc. | Texas |
| The Austin Diagnostic Clinic | Texas |

| | |
|---|---|
| The Medicus Firm | Texas |
| U.S. Physician Resources Intl Inc. | Texas |
| Uvalde Memorial Hospital | Texas |
| Valley Medical | Texas |
| Vitruvian Medical | Texas |
| Badmus Law Firm, PLLC | Texas |
| Columbia Healthcare | Utah |
| Commonwealth Physician Recruiting, Inc. | Virginia |
| JenCare Neighborhood Medical Centers | Virginia |
| Medical Staffing Associates, Inc. | Virginia |
| STG International | Virginia |
| VCU Health Systems/MCV Physicians | Virginia |
| Northwestern Medical Center | Vermont |
| Allen Cornelius Group, Inc. | Washington |
| Harrison Medical Center | Washington |
| MultiCare Provider Services | Washington |
| The Elliott Health Group, LLC | Washington |
| Concorde Staff Source | Wisconsin |
| Mercy Health System | Wisconsin |
| Strelcheck & Associates | Wisconsin |
| VISTA Staffing Solutions, Inc. | Wisconsin |
| Cabell Huntington Hospital, Inc. | West Virginia |
| Charleston Area Medical Center | West Virginia |

# Other Resources for IMGs Seeking Employment

- American College of Physicians: Career Opportunities
- Doctorwork.com
- Journal of the American Medical Association: CareerNet
- Monster Healthcare
- Physicians Employment
- Physicianwork.com
- PracticeLink

# Ethnic Medical Societies and Organizations

(Provided by the American Medical Association)

- Albanian American Medical Society
- American Association of Physicians of Indian Origin
- American College of International Physicians
- American Association of Surgeons of Indian Origin
- American Lebanese Medical Association
- Argentine - American Medical Society (AAMS)
- Asian-American Medical Society
- Association of Chinese American Physicians (ACAP)
- Association of Haitian Physicians Abroad
- Association of Kerala Medical Graduates
- Association of Nigerian Physicians in the Americas
- Association of Pakistani Physicians of North America
- Association of Philippine Physicians in America
- Bangladesh Medical Association of North America
- Burmese Medical Association of North American
- Chinese American Medical Society
- Chinese American Physicians' Society
- Confederation of Hispanic American Medical Associations
- Dominican American Medical Association of New York
- Hellenic Medical Society of Chicago
- Hellenic Medical Society of New York
- Hudson Valley Indian Physician Practitioners
- Hungarian Medical Association of America
- Illinois-Peruvian American Medical Society
- Indian American Urological Association
- Interamerican College of Physicians and Surgeons, Inc
- International College of Surgeons - U.S. Section
- Iranian American Medical Association
- Iranian Medical Society
- Islamic Medical Association of North America
- Japanese Medical Society of America
- Korean-American Medical Association of the U.S.
- Morgagni (Italian) Medical Society

- National Arab American Medical Association
- National Council of Asian & Pacific Islander Physicians
- National Hispanic Medical Association
- North American Taiwanese Medical Association-Chicago Chapter
- Peruvian American Medical Society
- Philippine Academy of Family Physicians
- Philippine Medical Association of America
- Polish-American Medical Society
- Rajasthan Medical Alumni Association
- Romanian Medical Society of New York
- Romanian Medical Association of America
- Russian American Medical Association
- Salvadorean American Medical Society
- Serbian-American Medical Society
- Society of Philippine Surgeons in America
- Spanish-American Medical Society
- Texas Association of Philippine Physicians
- Thai Physicians Association of America
- Turkish American Doctors Association of Midwest
- Ukrainian Medical Association of North American
- United States Colombian Medical Association (USCMA)
- Vietnamese Medical Association of the USA

## Board Certification Resources

- The American Board of Allergy and Immunology
- The American Board of Anesthesiology
- The American Board of Colon and Rectal Surgery
- The American Board of Dermatology
- The American Board of Emergency Medicine
- The American Board of Family Medicine
- The American Board of Internal Medicine
- The American Board of Medical Genetics
- The American Board of Neurological Surgery
- The American Board of Nuclear Medicine
- The American Board of Obstetrics and Gynecology

- <u>The American Board of Ophthalmology</u>
- <u>The American Board of Orthopedic Surgery</u>
- <u>The American Board of Otolaryngology</u>
- <u>The American Board of Pathology</u>
- <u>The American Board of Pediatrics</u>
- <u>The American Board of Physical Medicine and Rehabilitation</u>
- <u>The American Board of Plastic Surgery</u>
- <u>The American Board of Preventive Medicine</u>
- <u>The American Board of Psychiatry and Neurology</u>
- <u>The American Board of Radiology</u>
- <u>The American Board of Surgery</u>
- <u>The American Board of Thoracic Surgery</u>
- <u>The American Board of Urology</u>

# WORKS CITED

American College of Emergency Physicians. (2013). *Getting Sued: A Resident's Perspective*. Retrieved 2013, from ACEP.org: http://www.acep.org/content.aspx?id=22726

American College of Physicians. (n.d.). *Malpractice Insurance*. Retrieved 2013, from American College of Physicians: http://www.acponline.org/residents_fellows/career_counseling/malpractice_insurance.htm

American Medical Association. (2013). *IMG Resources*. Retrieved 2013, from American Medical Association: http://www.ama-assn.org/ama/pub/about-ama/our-people/member-groups-sections/international-medical-graduates/img-resources.page?

American Medical Association. (2013). *IMGs by Country of Origin*. Retrieved 2013, from American Medical Association: http://www.ama-assn.org/ama/pub/about-ama/our-people/member-groups-sections/international-medical-graduates/imgs-in-united-states/imgs-country-origin.page?

Brown, B. M. (2012). *The Deceptive Income of Physicians*. Retrieved 2013, from BenBrownMD: http://benbrownmd.wordpress.com/

Bureau of Labor Statistics. (2013). *Economy at a Glance*. Retrieved 2013, from BLS.gov: http://www.bls.gov/eag/eag.us.htm

Certification Matters. (2013). *About Board Certification.* Retrieved 2013, from Certification Matters: http://www. certificationmatters.org/about-board-certified-doctors/about-board-certification.aspx

Chua, Kao-Ping. (2006). *Overview of the U.S. Health Care System.* Retrieved 2013, from AMSA.

Falcon. (2011). *U.S. Residency Opportunities for International Medical Graduates.* Retrieved 2013, from Falcon: http:// www.falconreviews.com/v3/blog/2011/01/u-s-residency-opportunities-for-international-medical-graduates/

*GAO-10-412 Foreign Medical Schools: Education Should Improve Monitoring of Schools.* (2010). Retrieved 2013, from GAO.gov: http://www.gao.gov/assets/310/306027.html

Guey-Chi Chen, P. M. (2011). *Professional Challenges of Non-U.S.-Born International Medical Graduates and Recommendations of Support During Residency Training.* Retrieved 2013, from NIH Public Access: http://www.ncbi.nlm.nih.gov/pmc/articles/ PMC3257160/

Health Resources and Services Administration. (2013). *FAQ.* Retrieved 2013, from HRSA.gov: http://bhpr.hrsa.gov/shortage/ hpsas/faq.html

International Medical Graduates in American Medicine: Contemporary Challenges and Opportunities. (2010). Retrieved 2013, from American Medical Association.

Karnik, A. M. (2013). *International Medical Graduates - Training All Over Again.* Retrieved 2013, from American College of Physicians: http://www.acponline.org/about_acp/international/ graduates/training_in_us/karnik.htm

Medical News Today. (2012). *What is Medical Malpractice?* Retrieved 2013, from Medical News Today: http://www. medicalnewstoday.com/articles/248175.php

NAPR. (n.d.). *Job Search Resources.* Retrieved 2013, from National Association of Physcian Recruiters: http://www.napr. org/jobsearchresources.asp?login=false

Parasol. (n.d.). *Parasol.* Retrieved 2013, from Healthcare Needs of Customers: http://www.parasolfinancial.com/ Healthcare-Needs-Of-Your-Customers/

Pho, K. M. (2010). *International medical graduates and their patient outcomes.* Retrieved 2013, from KevinMD.com: http:// www.kevinmd.com/blog/2010/08/international-medical- graduates-patient-outcomes.html

PracticeLink. (2013). *Post-residency job hunting for the IMG.* Retrieved 2013, from PracticeLink: http://www.practicelink. com/magazine/legal-matters/post-residency-job-hunting- for-the-img/

PROFILES. (2012). *2011-2012 Physician Salary Survey.* Retrieved 2013, from Profiles: http://www.profilesdatabase.com/ resources/2011-2012-physician-salary-survey

Rampell, C. (2013, August). *Path to United States Practice is Long Slog to Foreign Doctors.* Retrieved 2013, from NYTimes. com: http://www.nytimes.com/2013/08/12/business/ economy/long-slog-for-foreign-doctors-to-practice-in-us. html?pagewanted=all&_r=1&

Sifferlin, A. (2012). *Doctors' Salaries: Who Earns the Most and the Least?* Retrieved 2013, from TIME: http://healthland. time.com/2012/04/27/doctors-salaries-who-earns-the- most-and-the-least/

Singer, P. N. (2008). *U.S. Tax Considerations for International Medical Students and Physicians.* Retrieved 2008, from FindLaw: http://corporate.findlaw.com/law-library/u-s-tax-considerations-for-international-medical-students-and.html

U.S. Department of Health and Human Services. (2013). *HRSA.* Retrieved 2013, from Find Shortage Areas: http://hpsafind.hrsa.gov/

United States Department of Health and Human Services. (2013). *GlobalHealth.* Retrieved from Global Health: http://www.globalhealth.gov/

Check the website (www.drsujansen.com) for other books of the series.

1. The Ultimate Career Guide for International Medical Graduates to Work in Canada.
2. The Ultimate Career Guide for International Medical Graduates to Work in the United Kingdom.
3. The Ultimate Career Guide for International Medical Graduates to Work in Australia.
4. The Ultimate Career Guide for International Medical Graduates to Work in New Zealand.
5. The Ultimate Career Guide for International Medical Graduates to Work in the Middle East Countries.

Printed in the United States
By Bookmasters